© Copyright 1978 by Greenhaven Press, Inc.

ISBN 0-912616-58-X Paper Edition
ISBN 0-912616-59-8 Cloth Edition

THE ISMS: MODERN DOCTRINES AND MOVEMENTS

Internationalism

Opposing Viewpoints

Bruno Leone

GREENHAVEN PRESS, INC.
1611 POLK ST. N.E.
MINNEAPOLIS, MINNESOTA 55413

SERIES EDITORS: DAVID L. BENDER AND GARY E. McCUEN

Contents

Internationalism

Exercises

Introduction

Albert Einstein once was asked to predict how World War III would be fought. After a thoughtful pause, he responded that he could not be certain about World War III. But the war following it, he said, "will be fought with stones."

There are few who would disagree with this ominous prediction. Owing to the nature of contemporary warfare, one day some may see Einstein's opinion actualized with a prophetic vengeance.

The search for a universal and lasting peace has been humankind's most formidable quest since recorded history. And despite its desirability, peace still remains our most elusive goal. One significant reason for this dilemma is our failure to see beyond the narrow limits of immediate allegiences. Attachments to Tribe, Church, and State tend to obscure the much broader ties of a common humanity.

Internationalism is the principle which seeks to inform people of these broader ties. It may be defined as a search for world order based on a belief in the essential unity of humankind. Most who support the principle view it as the only viable alternative to internecine warfare.

Since ancient times, internationalism has had many articulate and devoted spokespersons. According to his biographer, W. W. Tarn, Alexander the Great "prayed for a union of hearts" among people. He dreamed of a joint commonwealth in which former enemies would live in peace. St. Augustine reminded his contemporaries that national greatness was a passing thing. For Augustine, humankind's highest goal should be to attain oneness in the universal "City of God." Dante believed that unity was the constitutive principle of the universe. He wrote that just as the human body has one head, the world body politic also must be united under a single leader.

When the advent of gunpowder punctuated the toll and horrors of warfare, the number of internationalists increased correspondingly. And today, the portent of Armageddon has raised the cry for international concord to a missionary zeal.

While internationalism with its promise of peace is a tempting carrot to wave before the eyes of a war-weary world, the realization of a stable global order is questionable. International unity in a world of sovereign nations poses a legion of problems, the foremost being the question of what form that unity should take. Many internationalists support a loosely-knit federation of independent states cooperating, usually through an international agency, in matters of common interest. Others envision a One-World State, shorn of national boundaries and linguistic differences and both ruled and policed by a centralized executive body. There are, of course, numerous positions between these extremes.

Assuming a document of accord were promulgated, would the signatories to that agreement demonstrate the essential willingness to abide by the dictates of the majority, especially if that majority decision was deemed contrary to private national interests? The League of Nations and the United Nations are examples of the federated type of international body. Chauvinistic nationalism ultimately proved the death blow of the League, just as nationalism is seriously undermining the efficacy of the United Nations.

Harry S. Truman is quoted as saying, ''Our goal must be — not peace in our time — but peace for all time.'' Those sentiments have been uttered by internationalists with unceasing monotony through countless periods of war and peace. And still the question remains: will Internationalism ever become a true path to peace? Since history thus far has offered lamentably few favorable signs, one can only answer with the tired, worn, and familiar ''only time will tell.''

The following readings attempt to offer a cross-section of some of the political and philosophical arguments both for and against Internationalism. The reader should take careful note of the chapter on the League of Nations, as it portrays the difficulties which can arise when international interests conflict with national fears and ambitions.

Chapter 1

Internationalism

World Government: Peace or Despotism?

1

The Need for
World Government

W. Warren Wagar

A Fulbright Scholar and a PhD from Yale
University, W. Warren Wagar is Professor of
History at the State University of New York at
Binghamton. He has written and researched
extensively on the One World State. His works
include *The City of Man*, *Building the City of
Man* and *H.G. Wells and the World State*.

Consider the following questions while reading:

1. Why does Karl Jaspers suggest that no extraterrestrial life
   has made contact with us?
2. Why does the author feel that this is a key time during which
   to build a world civilization?

BUILDING A WORLD CIVILIZATION

All through history, men have responded to the collapse of old social orders by creating new social orders extensive enough to secure civil peace and humane values within the geographical limits of the society. In the present crisis, since here on earth geographical limits no longer exist, the only possible response true to man's nature as a social animal, is the building of a world civilization. If the response has succeeded before, on a continental scale, it can succeed again, on a planetary scale. Nothing at least absolutely vetoes it. The remedy must be as efficacious as ever.

A word of explanation. An organic world civilization is not a Utopia....It will be a world of finite men and women, no less corruptible than the men and women of imperial Rome, the Han and Gupta empires, or medieval Latin Christendom. It will draw deeply on the durable wisdom of the traditional civilizations, and it will share in their human shortcomings. But it must be a flourishing concern, a business in full operation, able to minister to the needs of all men, able to respond flexibly to new crises, able to grow and thrive in growing. It is the best form of life possible for mankind in an age of unlimited technics [technology] and a world community of peril. Its contours can only be guessed at, and yet it will not arrive by accident. In some never exactly foreseeable measure, to anticipate the future is to bring it under control.

AN AFFIRMATION OF HUMAN ONENESS

I am a member of the Family of Man.
My home is Earth.
The achievements of Mankind
throughout the ages are my heritage.
My destiny is bound to that of all my
fellow Human Beings.
What we jointly create forms
our bequest to future generations.
Let me do no harm to my Family.
Let us not do harm to those yet to come.

World Federalists Association

TIME IS GROWING SHORT

But we have long since passed the time when manly faith and simple courage in any quantity however great could guarantee us success. Because civilization-building takes centuries, and we may have only a few years left, it would be absurd to promise ourselves a happy ending in the tradition of fairy tales and celluloid melodramas. The wolves are not howling outside the ramparts of civilization: they have broken in. Their breath is hot on our cheeks. The human race has abruptly reached that unexpectedly dangerous stage in its evolution when it must live, and go on living for all time, with material means ready at hand to accomplish quickly and easily its total destruction. These material means will continue to increase in potency with each passing year. But the human beings who inherit this arsenal of ultimate weapons — biological, chemical, thermo-nuclear, radiological — will be in substance the same irritable

THERE OUGHT TO BE A LAW!

Justus in the **Minneapolis Star**. Reprinted by permission.

apes who first overran the planet only a few thousand years ago. They may grow in knowledge and strength, but they cannot entirely escape their instincts. Can men, remaining men, always through bluff or diplomacy or good sense somehow manage to avoid Armageddon? Karl Jaspers suggests that perhaps no extraterrestrial species has made contact with ours for the precise reason that no race can survive anywhere in the cosmos which has reached man's present level of technology. They all annihilate themselves in thermonuclear holocausts. And Jaspers, though hopeful, admits that our

Atomic cloud over Nagasaki, 20 minutes after blast on August 10, 194

survival is intellectually "improbable." In brief, we are guilty and doomed to die unless we can escape to the sanity of a new civilization built to the world scale of human intercourse...

POSTERITY DEMANDS IT

Whoever enlists in the cause of man in this age will find no time for nostalgia. We are the link between the traditional civilizations of a well remembered past and the emergent world civilization. We stand between. If we break under the strain, there will be no future. All posterity is in our keeping. Such a task against such towering odds joins man to man and weaves meaning into the vast fabric of confusion. It can be the difference between the life and death of the soul.

The Fantasy of World Government

Walter Berns

A noted educator and writer, Walter Berns received his PhD from the University of Chicago in 1950. He has taught at Louisiana University and Cornell University, where he was Chairman of the Department of Government from 1963 to 1968. Presently Professor of Political Science at the University of Toronto, he is the author of *Freedom, Virtue, and the First Amendment* and *Constitutional Cases in American Government*.

Consider the following questions while reading:

1. How does the author cite the United World Federalists as an example of the impossibility of world government?
2. How do U.S. and Soviet differences complicate the possibility of a world government?
3. Why does the author think that world despotism would result from world government?

Walter Berns, ''The Fantasy of World Government,'' **National Review**, April 22, 1961, pp. 245-46. Reprinted with permission from **National Review**, 150 East 35th St., New York, N.Y. 10016; $19.00 per year.

DISUNITED UNITED WORLD FEDERALISTS

It seems to me that the devotees of world government have minimized the difficulties involved; yet the experience of one of the major organizations devoted to the cause, the United World Federalists, points up these difficulties in a dramatic fashion. The members of the organization met and agreed, as one of them later reported, that ''a global government able to enforce law (in the sense of 'domestic law') on individual violators was necessary...and...possible...(and) that the only practicable form for such a world government was the federal form.'' But the members disagreed sharply on how to bring the world federation about, how to name the founding members, how to delegate powers to it. The members became ''enraged,'' accused each other of ''political immaturity,'' and demanded that the charters of affiliated groups be revoked. Finally, a deep schism left the parent organization with only half of its membership. The group that sought to unite the world could not even remain united itself.

WORLD GOVERNMENT AND TYRANNY

The character of a world government, represented today in essence by the United Nations is reactionary — a return to absolutism and totalitarianism so abhorred by those who for generations have fled from the tyrannical governments of the Old World. There is nothing to check the absolute power of world government, its decrees, its judgments; its legislative acts are final.

Mrs. Wilson K. Barnes, National Society, Daughters of the American Revolution, April 18, 1961.

A COMPLEX POLITICAL PROBLEM

How, then, can we get world government?

This, of course, is a political problem. The Soviet Union does not trust the West; the West, I hope, does not trust the Soviet Union. Whatever the chances of reaching agreement on some aspect of atomic disarmament, neither is likely to submit to a world government controlled by the other. Neither is likely to submit to a government controlled by others, if such a thing were possible, without the right to nullify decisions taken by these others. The example of the veto in the Security Council allows us to be as certain of this as we have to be. But the right to nullify decisions taken in important matters is incompatible with government.

Thus, the advocates of world government must explain how they intend to get the consent of the Soviet Union; for, even if the West believed in the necessity of world government, the political situation would be determined by the existence of a powerful Communist Russia rigidly controlled by a Central Committee that appears unlikely to agree to any non-Communist world government. There are two paths to consent: persuasion and force. The devotees of world government must get the consent of the Soviet Union by persuasion, but this seems impossible; or by force, which means, in the present state of armaments, by atomic war. But it is atomic war that we are trying to avoid!

It seems to me that the advocates of world government do not understand the political situation. To say, as Robert M. Hutchins does, that "men will fight until they get their rights," is to lose sight of the fact that men have also fought to get more than their rights, and, furthermore, overlooks the fact that men sometimes have peculiar notions as to their rights. Less than any generation in the history of the West can we deny that there are sometimes madmen in power who are willing to commit any crime at any cost, even at a cost involving the lives of millions of people, in the name of an unjust cause, which they, in their madness, call their rights.

The conclusion is this: we cannot persuade the Soviets to join a non-Communist world government; we cannot force them to join by any method short of atomic war; there can be no world government without them.

THE BOMB AND WORLD DESPOTISM
The usual objection to this analysis is that whatever the disagreements separating the United States and the Soviet Union, they are insignificant beside the massive agreement that there must be no atomic war. The threat of the bomb compels this agreement, and the agreement is the required foundation of world government. According to one of the world federalists

"the argument for world government is simple and irrefutable."

It is indeed simple, but it is not irrefutable. If the only agreement is the fear of atomic annihilation, the first concern of the world government must be to guard against the bomb. All the existing bombs, or at least all that are *supposed* to exist, will have been turned over to the World State to be guarded, somehow, someplace, by a mixed force of political janissaries — probably Swedes and Indians. But everyone will agree that this is not enough: it will also be necessary to guard against the future production of the bomb. This will require a police force, with the power to inspect everywhere at any time, and without a warrant. Its purpose will be to prevent the manufacture of the bomb and to ferret out potential manufacturers of the bomb — that is, anyone against whom there is the slightest suspicion. This will require eternal vigilance and rigorous methods. No world parliament can be allowed to filibuster while an accusation stands against one of the member states; it cannot be allowed in any way to stand against the swift intervention of the police force. The World Parliament would probably become the equivalent of the impotent Supreme Soviet; the head of the police force would probably have to intervene in the Parliament, shouting, as Cromwell did in another parliament, "Come, come, I will put an end to your prating." In short, world government based only on the fear of the bomb will be world despotism.

THE GREATER OF TWO EVILS

Even if we concede for a moment that this description of the world state is imaginary, we cannot, it seems to me, deny that it is possible. The question is, How *probable* is worldwide despotism? It seems especially probable if the threat of universal destruction is regarded as a greater evil than universal despotism, for this means that those who advocate world government will accept despotism in order to avoid destruction and, perhaps, even the threat of destruction. One is permitted to wonder whether that simple insight to which civilization is indebted — that there are greater evils than death and that there are some things for which men will give their lives — yet survives in modern man. Even we ought to know, as others knew 2,500 years ago, that fear is the principle of tyranny.

The Atomic Bomb and World Government

Albert Einstein

A native of Germany, Albert Einstein is most
noted for his theory of relativity, for which he
won the Nobel Prize in physics in 1921. Einstein
was a life long pacifist and advocate of Internationalism. His works in this area include
Why War? (in collaboration with Sigmund
Freud) and *The World as I See It*.

Consider the following questions while reading:

1. Why did Einstein suggest that Russia be invited to write the
   first draft of a world government constitution?
2. Why did Einstein recommend that the three great powers,
   united in a world government, have the right to intervene in
   the internal affairs of smaller countries?
3. Einstein did not see the minority government in Russia as a
   threat to world peace. What was his reasoning?
4. How did Einstein respond to the charge that world government could lead to world tyranny?

Albert Einstein, ''Einstein on the Atomic Bomb,'' **The Atlantic Monthly**, November 1945, pp.
43-45. Copyright © 1956, Estate of Albert Einstein. By permission of the Estate of Albert
Einstein.

WAR IS INEVITABLE

The release of atomic energy has not created a new problem. It has merely made more urgent the necessity of solving an existing one. One could say that it has affected us quantitatively, not qualitatively. As long as there are sovereign nations possessing great power, war is inevitable. That statement is not an attempt to say when war will come, but only that it is sure to come. That fact was true before the atomic bomb was made. What has been changed is the destructiveness of war.

I do not believe that civilization will be wiped out in a war fought with the atomic bomb. Perhaps two thirds of the people of the earth might be killed, but enough men capable of thinking, and enough books, would be left to start again, and civilization could be restored.

I do not believe that the secret of the bomb should be given to the United Nations organization. I do not believe that it should be given to the Soviet Union. Either course would be like the action of a man with capital, who, wishing another man to work with him on some enterprise, should start out by simply giving his prospective partner half of his money. The second man might choose to start a rival enterprise, when what was wanted was his cooperation.

BIG POWER COLLABORATION

The secret of the bomb should be committed to a World Government, and the United States should immediately announce its readiness to give it to a World Government. This government should be founded by the United States, the Soviet Union, and Great Britain — the only three powers with great military strength. All three of them should commit to this World Government all of their military strength. The fact that there are only three nations with great military power should make it easier rather than harder to establish such a government.

Since the United States and Great Britain have the secret of the atomic bomb and the Soviet Union does not, they should invite the Soviet Union to prepare and present the first draft of a Constitution for the proposed World Government. That action should help to dispel the distrust which the Russians already feel because the bomb is being kept a secret, chiefly to prevent their having it. Obviously the first draft would not be the final one, but the Russians should be made to feel that the World Government would assure them their security.

It would be wise if this Constitution were to be negotiated by a single American, a single Britisher, and a single Russian. They would have to have advisers, but these advisers should only advise when asked. I believe three men can succeed in writing a workable Constitution acceptable to all three nations. Six or seven men, or more, probably would fail.

SMALLER NATIONS TO FOLLOW

After the three great powers have drafted a Constitution and adopted it, the smaller nations should be invited to join the World Government. They should be free to stay out; and though they would be perfectly secure in staying out, I am sure they would wish to join. Naturally they should be entitled to propose changes in the Constitution as drafted by the Big Three. But the Big Three should go ahead and organize the World Government whether the smaller nations join or not.

ALLIANCE FOR PEACE

Since reason condemns war and makes peace an absolute duty, and since peace cannot be effected or guaranteed without a compact among nations, they must form an alliance of a peculiar kind, which may be called a pacific alliance, different from a treaty of peace, inasmuch as it would forever terminate all wars, whereas the latter only ends one.

Immanuel Kant, **Perpetual Peace**, 1795

The World Government would have power over all military matters and need have only one further power: the power to intervene in countries where a minority is oppressing a majority and creating the kind of instability that leads to war. Conditions such as exist in Argentina and Spain should be dealt with. There must be an end to the concept of non-intervention, for to end it is part of keeping the peace.

The establishment of the World Government must not have to wait until the same conditions of freedom are to be found in all three of the great powers. While it is true that in the Soviet Union the minority rules, I do not consider the internal conditions there are of themselves a threat to world peace. One must bear in mind that the people in Russia did not have a long political education, and changes to improve Russian conditions had to be carried through by a minority for the reason that there was no majority capable of doing it. If I had been born a Russian, I believe I could have adjusted myself to this condition.

It is not necessary, in establishing a world organization with a monopoly of military authority, to change the structure of the three great powers. It would be for the three individuals who draft the Constitution to devise ways for the different structures to be fitted together for collaboration.

THE LESSER OF TWO EVILS

Do I fear the tyranny of a World Government? Of course I do. But I fear still more the coming of another war or wars. Any government is certain to be evil to some extent. But a World Government is preferable to the far greater evil of wars, particularly with their intensified destructiveness. If a World Government is not established by agreement, I believe it will come in another way and in a much more dangerous form. For war or wars will end in one power's being supreme and dominating the rest of the world by its overwhelming military strength.

Now that we have the atomic secret, we must not lose it, and that is what we should risk doing if we should give it to the United Nations organization or to the Soviet Union. But we must make it clear, as quickly as possible, that we are not keeping the bomb a secret for the sake of our power, but in the hope of establishing peace in a World Government, and that we will do our utmost to bring this World Government into being.

TIME IS ESSENTIAL

I appreciate that there are persons who favor a gradual approach to World Government even though they approve of it as the ultimate objective. The trouble about taking little steps, one at a time, in the hope of reaching that ultimate goal is that while they are being taken, we continue to keep the bomb secret without making our reason convincing to those who do not have the secret. That of itself creates fear and suspicion, with the consequence that the relations of rival sovereignties deteriorate dangerously. So, while persons who take only a step at a time may think they are approaching world peace, they actually are contributing, by their slow pace, to the coming of war. We have no time to spend in this way. If war is to be averted, it must be done quickly.

'NOW, NOW! DON'T PANIC! AFTER I HAPPEN YOU WON'T FEEL A THING!'

We shall not have the secret very long. I know it is argued that no other country has money enough to spend on the development of the atomic bomb, and this fact assures us the secret for a long time. It is a mistake often made in this country to measure things by the amount of money they cost. But other countries which have the materials and the men can apply them to the work of developing atomic power if they care to do so. For men and materials and the decision to use them, and not money, are all that is needed...

I myself do not have the gift of explanation by which to persuade large numbers of people of the urgencies of the problems the human race now faces. Hence I should like to command someone who has this gift of explanation — Emery Reves, whose book, *The Anatomy of Peace*, is intelligent, brief, clear, and, if I may use the abused term, dynamic on the topic of war and the need for World Government.

Since I do not foresee that atomic energy is to be a great boon for a long time, I have to say that for the present it is a menace. Perhaps it is well that it should be. It may intimidate the human race into bringing order into its international affairs, which, without the pressure of fear, it would not do.

Einstein, the Big Powers, and World Government

Sumner Welles

A distinguished public servant and author, Sumner Welles was Ambassador to Cuba, Assistant Secretary of State and Under-Secretary of State during the administration of F. D. Roosevelt. He resigned from government in 1943 and devoted himself to lecturing and writing. He has authored *World of the Four Freedom* (1943), *The Time for Decision* (1944), and numerous other works.

Consider the following questions while reading:

1. Why did Ambassador Welles think Russia would not participate in a world government?
2. Why did he think Great Britain and the U.S. would be unwilling to join?
3. Why did the author claim that Einstein's proposed world government would lead to international serfdom?

Sumner Welles, ''The Atomic Bomb and World Government,'' **The Atlantic Monthly**, January 1946, pp. 39-41. Copyright © 1946 R 1974, by The Atlantic Monthly Company, Boston, Mass. Reprinted by permission.

EINSTEIN IS WRONG

In the November [1945] issue of *Atlantic Monthly*, Professor Albert Einstein has given us his drastic and urgent recommendations as to the course we should follow in dealing with the problem of the atomic bomb.

Professor Einstein has played a notable part in the development of atomic energy. He figured prominently in the series of events which led to the manufacture of the atomic bomb. He is a citizen of the United States, and his fellow Americans are justly proud of his achievements. I regret the obligation under which I find myself of taking issue with many of the views and recommendations set forth in his article. Yet I must do so because I believe that many people who recognize the authority with which he speaks in the field of science will be readily persuaded that he is for that reason an equally competent guide in the field of international politics...

Professor Einstein...asserts: "It is not necessary, in establishing a world organization with a monopoly of military authority, to change the structure of the three great powers. It would be for the three individuals who draft the constitution to devise ways for the different structures to be fitted together for collaboration."

In Professor Einstein's view the solution is as simple as that. He is evidently confident that adoption of his proposal is not only imperative but feasible as well.

The question before us is whether his proposal is practicable and desirable.

I am convinced that the achievement of any such objective at this time is wholly impracticable. I must add that I also have grave questions as to the desirability of his proposal in the form in which he presents it.

RUSSIA WOULD NOT PARTICIPATE

Professor Einstein's concept is premised upon his assumption that the Soviet Government would agree to a world government with power "over all military matters" provided the Soviet Government may prepare the first draft of a constitution for such a world government.

It is interesting to speculate as to the nature of the draft constitution which the Soviet Government would now prepare.

I can conceive of the Soviet Union's agreeing to enter a world government if a constitution is drafted, and is agreed upon by the United States and Great Britain, which provides for a World Union of Soviet Socialist Republics with the capital of that world government located in Moscow. I cannot imagine that the Soviet Union would participate in a world government upon any other basis.

No world government of the character envisaged by Professor Einstein could function unless it possessed the power to

Albert Einstein in 1953

Wide World Photos

exercise complete control over the armaments of each constituent state, and unless every nation was willing to open up every inch of its territory and every one of its laboratories and factories to a continuing international inspection. Nor could it function unless the government of each participating country was equally willing to submit to the scrutiny of the authorities of the world government every one of its governmental processes, including its conduct of foreign and internal affairs and of finance.

It surely requires no demonstration that any such requisite as that would wholly destroy the present Soviet system. We have every right to believe, from our knowledge of Russian policy and from our understanding of the fundamental motives inherent in the Soviet form of Communism, that neither the present Soviet Government nor the rank and file of the members of the Communist Party in Russia would ever consent to the obliteration, from one day to another, of the system which, over a period of twenty-eight years, they have at so great a sacrifice finally, with a great measure of success, established. We have every reason to be confident that unless the Soviet Union could so dominate the proposed world government as to preclude the possibility of any weakening of its own control of Russian foreign and domestic policy, it would not participate in that government.

DIFFERENCES ARE TOO GREAT
And what about the United States and Great Britain?

We may, for the sake of argument, grant the highly unlikely possibility that a majority of the people of the United States would be willing to consider participation in a United States of the World built upon a foundation similar to that provided in their own Federal Constitution. It is within the realm of possibility that the British people would be willing to throw overboard their own form of government, although it has served them well and proved responsive to their own peculiar requirements, and join in such a United States of the World. But it is to my mind fantastic to assume that either the American or the British people would be willing to join in a World Union of Soviet Socialist Republics when such a union would inevitably result in the dissolution of the individual form of government which they have gradually evolved to meet their national needs, and also abolish all those cherished principles of individual liberty which are sacred to the Anglo-Saxon peoples — and which, in the case of the United States, are comprised in the Bill of Rights.

I believe that the major fallacy in Professor Einstein's proposal lies in his assertion that "it is not necessary, in establishing a world organization with a monopoly of military authority, to change the structure of the three great powers." I regard it as wholly impossible that the three individuals who, he suggests, should draft the constitution for this world government could, for the purposes he envisages, ever succeed in devising "ways for the different structures to be fitted together for collaboration."

TOO HIGH A COST

There is another aspect of Professor Einstein's proposal which fills me with amazement. He declares that, in addition to the other powers with which he would vest his world government, that government should have " the power to intervene in countries where a minority is oppressing a majority and creating the kind of instability that leads to war." He admits that it is true that in the Soviet Union the minority rules, but he insists that, if he had been born a Russian, he could have "adjusted" himself to this condition.

If I understand his thesis correctly, and I think I do, minority rule should be regarded as iniquitous in every nation of the world except the Soviet Union. His proposed world government would, therefore, be granted the right to intervene in every country of the earth for the purpose of establishing there such form of government, or such internal regime, as the dominating powers within the world government considered desirable, with the exception of the Soviet Union.

This view, of course, approximates the classic thesis of the Third International that minorities are entitled to exercise control when they are of the Communist faith. Examples are not wanting that the logical outgrowth of this philosophy is the assertion of the right of Communist minorities by liquidations and terror to dominate opposing majorities until those majorities have been forced into the Communist line.

The issue raises one of the gravest problems with which freedom-loving people are today faced. Will peoples such as the English-speaking peoples, determined upon the preservation at any cost of their individual liberty, accept any form of world order which grants to some alien and superior power the authority to intervene in their internal life in such a manner as to determine for them how they shall be governed, to what extent their individual liberty may be reduced, and whether the voice of dissenting minorities or of dissenting majorities may make itself heard?

INTERNATIONAL SERFDOM

I wholly agree that no peaceful world can be envisaged unless the nations which take part in a new international organization voluntarily fix certain standards of governmental conduct which they commit themselves severally to uphold. These standards must comprehend the assurance that religious and political freedom, and the chance to obtain economic security, will be guaranteed without discrimination to all their respective nationals. This international organization must see to it that the guaranties so fixed are carried out.

But any intervention, such as that which Professor Einstein proposes, upon the part of his world government, in the internal affairs of independent peoples, for the sole purpose of imposing upon them a standardized form of government or a particular brand of political philosophy, would subject the nations of the world to a dictatorship exercised by the Big Three, with all other peoples as abject serfs. No free world can be founded upon a such a concept. It was precisely in order to prevent the establishment of such a world that the vast majority of the United Nations fought through to final victory over the Axis powers.

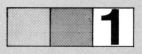
Fact and Opinion

This discussion exercise is designed to promote experimentation with one's ability to distinguish between fact and opinion. It is a fact, for example, that the United States was militarily involved in the Vietnam War. But to say that this involvement served the interests of world peace is an opinion or conclusion. Future historians will agree that American soldiers fought in Vietnam, but their interpretations about the causes and consequences of the war will probably vary greatly.

Consider each statement carefully. Mark (O) for any statement you feel is an opinion or interpretation of the facts. Mark (F) for any statement you believe is fact. Then discuss and compare your judgments with those of other class members.

O = OPINION
F = FACT

_____ 1. The United States must always be the most powerful nation.

_____ 2. We must end military and arms sales to foreign nations because both activities promote war and violence.

_____ 3. The United States should give first priority to negotiating a reduction in nuclear arms with the Russians.

_____ 4. We must never negotiate with the Russians since they cannot be trusted.

_____ 5. We must be willing to accept military parity with the Russians or no arms reduction will ever take place.

_____ 6. There should be a world government to guarantee the welfare of all countries.

23

_____ 7. We should not cooperate in world economic agreements that do not further American economic prosperity.

_____ 8. People should seek world citizenship at the expense, if necessary, of national citizenship.

_____ 9. The United States should refuse to cooperate in any total disarmament program.

_____ 10. We must never participate in any international organization that requires us to give up any of our national rights and freedom of action.

_____ 11. An international police force should be the only organization in the world allowed to have armaments.

_____ 12. All national governments should be abolished and replaced by one central world government.

_____ 13. War is simply murder carried out by nations.

_____ 14. War is sometimes a good way to solve international problems.

_____ 15. Dispute between nations should be settled without war.

_____ 16. There would be little progress without war.

_____ 17. War develops moral strength.

_____ 18. Everyone should refuse to participate in any war.

_____ 19. It is hard to decide whether wars promote more good than harm.

_____ 20. Fighting for one's country is a person's highest duty.

Chapter 2

Internationalism

The League of Nations:

Yesterday's Path to Peace?

The League of Nations: Insurance Against War

Woodrow Wilson

The League of Nations was the brainchild of President Woodrow Wilson. Wilson was convinced that the League represented humankind's one hope of preventing another war of the magnitude of World War I. Faced with mounting congressional opposition to America's entry into the League, he brought his case before the electorate in a series of coast to coast speeches. Wilson argued that it was morally imperative that the United States become a signatory to the Covenant of the League. With typical idealism, he expressed faith in the belief that once the nations of the world were united in an international organization dedicated to peace, they would surely act in concert to preserve that peace. The following was a speech delivered at Pueblo, Colorado on September 25, 1919.

Consider the following questions while reading:

1. What method did President Wilson suggest the League of Nations use to prevent war between belligerent nations?
2. What argument did he present to urge the United States to join the League of Nations?

President Woodrow Wilson in a speech delivered at Pueblo, Colorado on September 25, 1919.

A FALSE IMPRESSION OF THE LEAGUE

The chief pleasure of my trip has been that it has nothing to do with my personal fortunes, that it has nothing to do with my personal reputation, that it has nothing to do with anything except great principles uttered by Americans of all sorts and of all parties which we are now trying to realize at this crisis of the affairs of the world. But there have been unpleasant impressions as well as pleasant impressions, my fellow citizens, as I have crossed the continent. I have perceived more and more that men have been busy creating an absolutely false impression of what the treaty of peace and the covenant of the league of nations contain and mean...

PREAMBLE TO THE COVENANT OF THE LEAGUE OF NATIONS — 1919

THE HIGH CONTRACTING PARTIES,

In order to promote international cooperation and to achieve international peace and security
by the acceptance of obligations not to resort to war,
by the prescription of open, just and honorable relations between nations,
by the firm establishment of the understandings of international law as the actual rule of conduct among Governments,
and by the maintenance of justice and a scrupulous respect for all treaty obligations in the dealings of organised peoples with one another,

Agree to this Covenant of the League of Nations.

UNITED MORAL FORCES OF THE WORLD

At the front of this great treaty is put the covenant of the league of nations. It will also be at the front of the Austrian treaty and the Hungarian treaty and the Bulgarian treaty and the treaty with Turkey. Every one of them will contain the covenant of the league of nations, because you can not work any of them without the covenant of the league of nations. Unless you get

the united, concerted purpose and power of the great Governments of the world behind this settlement, it will fall down like
a house of cards. There is only one power to put behind the
liberation of mankind, and that is the power of mankind. It is
the power of the united moral forces of the world, and in the
covenant of the league of nations the moral forces of the world
are mobilized. For what purpose? Reflect, my fellow citizens,
that the membership of this great league is going to include all
the great fighting nations of the world, as well as the weak
ones. It is not for the present going to include Germany, but for
the time being Germany is not a great fighting country. All the
nations that have power that can be mobilized are going to be
members of this league, including the United States. And what
do they unite for? They enter into a solemn promise to one
another that they will never use their power against one
another for aggression; that they never will impair the territorial integrity of a neighbor; that they never will interfere with
the political independence of a neighbor; that they will abide by
the principle that great populations are entitled to determine
their own destiny and that they will not interfere with that
destiny; and that no matter what differences arise amongst
them they will never resort to war without first having done one
or the other of two things — either submitted the matter of
controversy to arbitration, in which case they agree to abide by
the result without question, or submitted it to the consideration
of the council of the league of nations, laying before that
council all the documents, all the facts, agreeing that the
council can publish the documents and the facts to the whole
world, agreeing that there shall be six months allowed for the

DEMOCRATS FAVOR LEAGUE

The Democratic party favors the League of Nations as the
surest, if not the only practicable means of maintaining the
peace of the world and terminating the insufferable burden of
great military and naval establishments. It was for this that
America broke away from traditional isolation and spent her
blood and treasure to crush a colossal scheme of conquest.

Democratic National Platform, 1920

mature consideration of those facts by the council, and
agreeing that at the expiration of the six months, even if they
are not then ready to accept the advice of the council with.
regard to the settlement of the dispute, they will still not go to
war for another three months. In other words, they consent, no
matter what happens, to submit every matter of difference
between them to the judgment of mankind, and just so
certainly as they do that, my fellow citizens, war will be in the
far background, war will be pushed out of that foreground of
terror in which it has kept the world for generation after

**The "Big Four"— Wilson, Orlando, Clemenceau,
and Lloyd George at Versailles in 1919**

generation, and men will know that there will be a calm time of deliberate counsel. The most dangerous thing for a bad cause is to expose it to the opinion of the world. The most certain way that you can prove that a man is mistaken is by letting all his neighbors know what he thinks, by letting all his neighbors discuss what he thinks, and if he is in the wrong you will notice that he will stay at home, he will not walk on the street. He will be afraid of the eyes of his neighbors. He will be afraid of their judgment of his character. He will know that his cause is lost unless he can sustain it by the arguments of right and of justice. The same law that applies to individuals applies to nations...

NO MORE WAR

I am dwelling upon these points, my fellow citizens, in spite of the fact that I dare say to most of you they are perfectly well

THE ACCUSER

known, because in order to meet the present situation we have got to know what we are dealing with. We are not dealing with the kind of document which this is represented by some gentlemen to be; and inasmuch as we are dealing with a document simon-pure in respect of the very principles we have professed and lived up to, we have got to do one or other of two things — we have got to adopt it or reject it. There is no middle course. You can not go in on a special-privilege basis of your own. I take it that you are too proud to ask to be exempted from responsibilities which the other members of the league will carry. We go in upon equal terms or we do not go in at all; and if we do not go in, my fellow citizens, think of the tragedy of that result — the only sufficient guaranty to the peace of the world withheld! Ourselves drawn apart with that dangerous pride which means that we shall be ready to take care of ourselves, and that means that we shall maintain great standing armies and an irresistible navy; that means we shall have the organization of a military nation; that means we shall have a general staff, with the kind of power that the general staff of Germany had, to mobilize this great manhood of the Nation when it pleases, all the energy of our young men drawn into the thought and preparation for war. What of our pledges to the men that lie dead in France? We said that they went over there, not to prove the prowess of America or her readiness for another war but to see to it that there never was such a war again. It always seems to make it difficult for me to say anything, my fellow citizens, when I think of my clients in this case. My clients are the children; my clients are the next generation. They do not know what promises and bonds I undertook when I ordered the armies of the United States to the soil of France, but I know, and I intend to redeem my pledges, to the children; they shall not be sent upon a similar errand.

The League of Nations: An Entangling Foreign Involvement

Henry Cabot Lodge

Lawyer, historian, and U.S. Senator from
Massachusetts, Henry Cabot Lodge was largely
responsible for America's failure to ratify the
Treaty of Versailles and gain entry into the
League of Nations. As Senate Majority Leader
and Chairman of the Senate Committee on
Foreign Relations, Lodge effectively stymied
Wilson's campaign to gain popular support for
admission into the League. An avowed isola-
tionist, he later led the opposition to President
Harding's plan for a World Court. Lodge was a
prolific author whose works included bio-
graphies of American leaders such as George
Washington, Alexander Hamilton, and Daniel
Webster.

Consider the following questions while reading:

1. Why did Senator Lodge think it was in the world's best
   interest for the United States not to join the League?
2. What reasons did Senator Lodge advance in arguing that the
   United States should not join the League of Nations?

Henry Cabot Lodge in a speech delivered in the U.S. Senate on August 12, 1919.

AVOID FOREIGN INVOLVEMENTS

We ought to reduce to the lowest possible point the foreign questions in which we involve ourselves. Never forget that this league is primarily — I might say overwhelmingly — a political organization, and I object strongly to having the politics of the United States turn upon disputes where deep feeling is aroused but in which we have no direct interest. It will all tend to delay the Americanization of our great population, and it is more important not only to the United States but to the peace of the world to make all these people good Americans than it is to determine that some piece of territory should belong to one European country rather than to another. For this reason I wish to limit strictly our interference in the affairs of Europe and of Africa. We have interests of our own in Asia and in the Pacific which we must guard upon our own account, but the less we undertake to play the part of umpire and thrust ourselves into European conflicts the better for the United States and for the world.

PROTECT OUR INDEPENDENCE

It has been reiterated here on this floor, and reiterated to the point of weariness, that in every treaty there is some sacrifice of sovereignty. That is not a universal truth by any means, but it is true of some treaties and it is a platitude which does not require reiteration. The question and the only question before us here is how much of our sovereignty we are justified in sacrificing. In what I have already said about other nations putting us into war I have covered one point of sovereignty which ought never to be yielded — the power to send American soldiers and sailors everywhere, which ought never to be taken from the American people or impaired in the slightest degree. Let us beware how we palter with our interdependence. We have not reached the great position from which we were able to come down into the field of battle and help to save the world from tyranny by being guided by others. Our vast power has all been built up and gathered together by ourselves alone. We forced our way upward from the days of the Revolution, through a world often hostile and always indifferent. We owe no debt to anyone except to France in that Revolution, and those policies and those rights on which our power has been founded should never be lessened or weakened. It will be no

service to the world to do so and it will be of intolerable injury
to the United States. We will do our share. We are ready and
anxious to help in all ways to preserve the world's peace. But
we can do it best by not crippling ourselves.

REPUBLICANS AGAINST LEAGUE

**The Republican party maintains the traditional American
policy of noninterference in the political affairs of other
nations. This government has definitely refused membership
in the League of Nations and to assume any obligations under
the covenant of the League. On this we stand.**

Republican National Platform, 1928

A SINGLE ALLEGIANCE

I am as anxious as any human being can be to have the United
States render every possible service to the civilization and the
peace of mankind, but I am certain we can do it best by not
putting ourselves in leading strings or subjecting our policies
and our sovereignty to other nations. The interdependence of
the United States is not only more precious to ourselves but to
the world than any single possession...Contrast the United
States with any country on the face of the earth today and ask
yourself whether the situation of the United States is not the
best to be found. I will go as far as anyone in the world service
but the first step to world service is the maintenance of the
United States. You may call me selfish, if you will, conservative
or reactionary, or use any other harsh adjective you see fit to
apply, but an American I was born, an American I have
remained all my life. I can never be anything else but an
American, and I must think of the United States first, and when
I think of the United States first in an arrangement like this I
am thinking of what is best for the world, for if the United
States fails the best hopes of mankind fail with it. I have never
had but one allegiance — I can not divide it now. I have loved
but one flag and I can not share that devotion and give affection
to the mongrel banner invented for a league. Internationalism,
illustrated by the Bolshevik and by the men to whom all
countries are alike provided they can make money out of them,
is to me repulsive. National I must remain, and in that way I

like all other Americans can render the amplest service to the world. The United States is the world's best hope, but if you fetter her in the interests and quarrels of other nations, if you tangle her in the intrigues of Europe, you will destroy her power for good and endanger her very existence. Leave her to march freely through the centuries to come as in the years that have gone...

LET THE LEAGUE PERISH

We are told that we shall "break the heart of the world" if we do not take this league just as it stands. I fear that the hearts of the vast majority of mankind would beat on strongly and steadily and without any quickening if the league were to perish altogether. If it should be effectively and beneficiently changed the people who would lie awake in sorrow for a single right could be easily gathered in one not very large room but those who would draw a long breath of relief would reach to millions.

We hear much of visions and I trust we shall continue to have visions and dream dreams of a fairer future for the race. But visions are one thing and visionaries are another, and the mechanical appliances of the rhetorician designed to give a picture of a present which does not exist and of a future which no man can predict are as unreal and short lived as the steam or canvas clouds, the angels suspended on wires and the artificial lights of the stage. They pass with the moment of effect and are shabby and tawdry in the daylight. Let us at least be real. Washington's entire honesty of mind and his fearless look into the face of all facts are qualities which can never go out of fashion and which we should all do well to imitate.

Ideals have been thrust upon us as an argument for the league until the healthy mind which rejects can't revolt from them...

AMERICA FIRST

No doubt many excellent and patriotic people see a coming fulfillment of noble ideals in the words "League for Peace." We all respect and share these aspirations and desires, but some of us see no hope, but rather defeat, for them in this murky covenant. For we, too, have our ideals, even if we differ from those who have tried to establish a monopoly of idealism.

Our first ideal is our country, and we see her in the future, as in the past, giving service to all her people and to the world. Our ideal of the future is that she should continue to render that service of her own free will. She has great problems of her own to solve, very grim and perilous problems, and a right solution, if we can attain to it, would largely benefit mankind. We would have our country strong to resist a peril from the West, as she has flung back the German menace from the East. We would not have our politics distracted and embittered by the dissensions of other lands. We would not have our country's vigor exhausted, or her moral force abated, by everlasting meddling and muddling in every quarrel, great and small, which afflicts the world.

INTERRUPTING THE CEREMONY

The League of Nations:
An Agency of Conciliation

Clarence K. Streit

A newspaper columnist and author, Clarence K.
Streit has long been an advocate of World
Government. He graduated from Montana State
University and attended Oxford University in
1920 and 1921 on a Rhodes Scholarship. From
1925 to 1939, he was the New York Times
League of Nations and Washington Bureau
correspondent. His books include *Freedom
Against Itself* and *The New Federalist*.

Consider the following questions:

1. Why does the author compare the League of Nations to a
   flying machine?
2. How does Mr. Streit respond to criticisms of the League?

Clarence K. Streit, ''The World's Efforts to Attain Peace,'' **New York Times Magazine**, August
12, 1934. © 1934 by The New York Times Company. Reprinted by permission.

THE WORLD BEFORE THE LEAGUE

There was no League of Nations on this day twenty years ago, when Germany was completing the subjugation of Belgium and preparing to invade France in force. Men had dreamed for thousands of years of stopping war, just as they had dreamed of flying. By 1914, they had discovered a way to fly, though the machinery was crude, dangerous. Often it killed. But sometimes it worked. There was not even crude machinery in 1914 for preventing war.

There were, it is true, these time-tried methods: armaments and Ambassadors, secret arming and secret diplomacy. But these were designed not to make peace but to win wars, to keep not peace but truces so long as they were advantageous.

There were some arbitration treaties, but they carefully reserved to the ordeal of war the settlement of all disputes involving ''national honor'' or ''vital interests.'' There had been speeches from time to time in favor of a World Court. A peace congress had met at The Hague in 1907, but nothing had been done in seven years to remedy its failure.

No government was under any obligation to try to settle without bloodshed any serious dispute, or even to consult face to face with other governments. Indeed, as Sir Edward Grey found to his and mankind's grief, merely to seek to improvise at the last hour a conference to prevent war was worse than vain.

No one knew in 1914 that war in four years could kill 13,000,000 men all round the world. War then was not the most abominable of crimes. It was no crime at all. It was the field of honor. There was everything designed to make war. There was nothing designed to prevent it.

THE WORLD SINCE THE LEAGUE

Now, twenty years after, neither this nor its reverse is true. There is still danger of war. There is still everything to make war. But now there are some things to prevent it, some things designed solely to keep peace — not things like War Offices and Foreign Offices, for which ''peace'' is sometimes a by-product. The new peace machinery is as crude, measured by the job it is designed to do, as was the flying machinery of twenty years ago. It has not yet gone round the world. It has not always worked. But it has worked sometimes.

CIVILIZED NATIONS SHOULD COMBINE

The one effective move for obtaining peace is by an agreement among all the great powers in which each should pledge itself not only to abide by the decisions of a common tribunal but to back its decisions by force. The great civilized nations should combine by solemn agreement in a great world league for the peace of righteousness.

Theodore Roosevelt

First in time and foremost in importance among the devices primarily for the preservation of peace is the League of Nations. It seeks to do its work through the organs it has created and the obligations its members have accepted. Its aim is to prevent all international conflicts, including those involving national honor, vital interests and treaty revision. It seeks continuous cooperation before conflict comes for the peaceful settlement of disputes, once they arise, by conciliation, private consultation, public conference, judicial decision, arbitration; and for the maintenance by force — moral, economic or military — of a system of law against those who refuse to respect it otherwise.

The League organs — Assembly, Council, Secretariat, International Labor Organization, Permanent Court for International Justice, economic, financial, transit, health, information and education sections — are numerous, permanent, with a proved capacity for growth. The League obligations, though leaving some loopholes for war, are comprehensive.

The League covenant no longer stands alone. There is a peace pact by which some sixty governments declare war a crime, renounce it as an instrument of national policy and pledge themselves to settle all disputes peacefully. The pact is more drastic in its undertaking than the covenant, but it has no machinery for its execution. It depends for execution on the circumstance that all the important States that are bound to use the covenant's execution machinery have bound themselves also to the pact's objectives, and two more States besides, the United States and Soviet Russia.

Nor is this all the peace machinery that has developed in the past twenty years. There are the Washington treaties — Naval, Nine-Power, Four-Power — the Locarno treaty, the London naval treaty, the optional clause by which twoscore governments have opted for the compulsory jurisdiction of the World Court, the general act by which a score of them have tightened the obligatory character of conciliation or arbitration for disputes among them. There are hundreds of bilateral treaties for conciliation, arbitration, judicial settlement, non-aggression.

The peace machinery that has developed since 1914 is far more comprehensive than many realize. Since it began with the adoption of the covenant there have been more threats of war, if anything, than ever before — for a great fire leaves many sparks. But since then not one big war has been declared. There has been fighting, but the hostilities have been minor affairs compared even with the Balkan Wars, the Russo-Japanese War and the Spanish-American War — the kind of thing that was breaking out somewhere in the world every five or ten years before the League began functioning. Yet there is now widespread through the world a feeling of disillusionment often bordering on despair regarding the League and all this peace machinery.

Certainly the League has not measured up to the great hopes entertained for such an organization in the days of the "war to end war," the "war to make the world safe for democracy." It apparently seems to many in retrospect that the whole war was fought solely and consciously to create the League. One gets the impression from the way people now voice their disappointment in the League — the bitter-enders then being naturally most bitterly disillusioned now — that it was the League which filled the front page during the war and during the peace conference, and that everything since then had centred on perfecting the peace machinery.

The disillusionment, in fact, seems to be at least partly due to a curiously widespread illusion. It seems to have been completely forgotten that the League of Nations was so much the poor relation of the peace conference that the commission which drafted the covenant had to sit mostly after office hours. President Wilson alone among the great-power leaders attended its meetings; such statesmen as Lloyd George and Clemenceau did not have time to bother with making machinery for preventing the slaughter of another 13,000,000 men...

CRITICISM OF THE LEAGUE

It was not generally expected of the Wright brothers that they prove the value of their flying machine by flying around the world or even across the Atlantic the first time they left the ground. The marvel was that they could stay in the air at all. But did people marvel when the new peace machinery actually

THE LEAGUE OF NATIONS ARGUMENT IN A NUTSHELL

Ding, J. N. (Ding) Darling Foundation

stopped war between Greece and Bulgaria? Or did they belittle this achievement and the peaceful settlement of the Mosul question, the Austro-German customs protocol, the Anglo-Persian oil dispute, the hostilities between Peru and Colombia?

Do or do not people now condemn the League as a hopeless failure because it has not kept a great military power out of Manchuria; because it has not already remedied all the mistakes made at Versailles; because it has not cured the world's economic, monetary and armament ills at the first world conferences ever assembled to cure them? It is generally held that its failures have, after all, cost relatively few lives and given invaluable lessons for strengthening its machinery? Or is the notion widespread that because of its failures and because its writ cannot yet be trusted to run around the world the League should be thrown on the ash-heap; that men should stick entirely to the old-fashioned ways of secret armaments and secret diplomacy?

If one asks, whether in France, England or America, the reason for disappointment in the League, for belief in the dismal failure of the peace machinery, the answer usually is that the Disarmament Conference has not yet brought security (say the French) or disarmament (say the English and Americans). And all answer that the League and the peace pact and the Nine-Power treaty failed to meet the Japanese test. The conclusion, is drawn that all this peace machinery put together cannot be trusted to prevent that "next great war" which is forever alarming the war-shocked generation of 1914-18.

If one questions further, all the complaints of people against the League and other peace machinery seem everywhere to boil down to this: the League is too weak, too slow, too cumbersome. People talk of it exactly as they talked of Congress under the Articles of Confederation: "It can declare anything, but it can do nothing."

This criticism seems especially to prevail among Americans. There was a time when many people everywhere feared the League would be too powerful. That was precisely why the drafters of its covenant saddled it with such devices as the unanimity rule, whereby any single sovereign State can legally block action. They were more concerned at the start with the brakes than with the motor.

THE LEAGUE MUST BE GIVEN A CHANCE

There was a time when, despite the fifty-nation-power brakes on a one-nation-power motor, Americans refused to go into Wilson's League or lend it any of their strength because they thought it was too strong, a "super-State." There was a time — merely six years ago — when irreconcilable American Senators consented to the peace pact only because they considered it a pious wish." Now it seems Americans in one breath condemn the League as being hopelessly supine and in the next breath refuse to strengthen it by supplying the missing part which American entry alone can supply — for, after all, this League mechanism was designed by an American to function with the United States as one of its essential cogs.

The question seems to be whether the old fear that the League is too strong will kill it or whether the new fear that it is too weak will cause it to be made stronger.

If the despondent character of the talk of the day is the only clue to the future of the League, then the outlook is black. But if the development of machinery in the realm of transportation gives any indication, it is not so dark. People held mass meetings against that devilish contrivance of Stephenson's that hurtled man along at the "frightful" speed of fifteen miles an hour. But people did not go back to the stage-coach. They went on to the airplane.

Political machinery, of course, may evolve differently. So far, however, its evolution seems to have followed the same general line. The American Union certainly was not born full-fledged. It first grew through the Confederation. The Articles of Confederation gave Congress hardly more power than the covenant gives the League. Yet it took years to get the thirteen States to ratify these articles, even while they were fighting together against England, because people thought the articles created a super-State dangerous to their individual freedom.

But when experience proved that the articles were too weak, when the thirteen sovereign States fell a prey to worse and worse economic, financial and social ills culminating in Shay's

Rebellion, when people began to believe that the danger to their freedom lay in the weakness of this American league, they did not scrap the Confederation and turn backward. They went on and made so strong a Union that their own only war among themselves thereafter was to prove that it could keep its members from seceding from it.

The "failure" of the League may result otherwise, but only if history does not repeat itself.

The Defense of the German State

Adolf Hitler

The League of Nations began suffering serious
setbacks during the 1930s. In September, 1931,
Japan initiated an unprovoked attack against
Chinese forces in Manchuria. Within two years
of the invasion, Japan formally resigned from
the League. In October, 1933, Germany also
withdrew from the League after walking out of a
world disarmament conference being held at
Geneva, Switzerland.

An air of crisis began developing in Europe and
many nations, such as Russia and France,
reacted by strengthening their armed forces.
Responding in kind, Germany proclaimed
universal military conscription on March 16,
1935. Among its other provisions, the proclama-
tion provided for a ''peacetime'' army of
324,000 men (excluding naval and air forces). In
the following speech, Adolf Hitler attempted to
justify the new law on the grounds of national
defense and integrity.

Consider the following question while reading:

1. What did Hitler claim was Germany's primary reason for
   wanting to increase its power?

From **The Speeches of Adolf Hitler** edited by Norman H. Baynes Vol. II. Reprinted by permission of Oxford University Press, (1942).

GERMANY DESIRES PEACE

The German Government was forced of its own motion to take the necessary measures to bring to an end the unworthy and in the last resort menacing state of powerless defencelessness of a great people and Reich.

In this the Government was influenced by the same considerations as those which Mr. Baldwin so truly expressed in his last speech: ''A country which shows itself unwilling to make what necessary preparations are requisite for its own defence will never have force, moral or material, in this world.''

But the Government of the German Reich of to-day desires only a single moral and material power — that is the power to be able to safeguard peace for the Reich and thereby for the whole of Europe.

WE WANT PEACE

I am not so senseless as to want war. We want peace and understanding, nothing else. We want to give our hand to our former enemies...when has the German people ever broken its word?

Adolf Hitler, 1933.

It has therefore taken all further steps which lay within its power which might serve to advance the cause of peace:

1. It has for a long time past offered to all neighbouring States the conclusion of pacts of non-aggression.

2. With its neighbouring State on the East (Poland) it has sought and found a treaty arrangement which, thanks to ready understanding on the part of that State, has, the Government hopes for all time, cleared the poisonous and threatening atmosphere which it found in existence when it came into power and which will lead to a permanent understanding and friendship between the two peoples.

3. Finally it has given to France the solemn assurance that

Germany, now that the question of the Saar has been settled, will not make or raise any further territorial claims on France...

EUROPE IS REARMING

The German Government must, however, to its regret, observe that for months past there has been taking place a continuous increase in armaments on the part of the rest of the world. It sees in the creation of a Soviet-Russian army of 101 divisions i.e. an admitted peace-strength of 960,000 men, an element that could not have been contemplated at the time of the conclusion of the Treaty of Versailles.

It sees in the speeding-up of similar measures in other States further proofs of the rejection of the idea of the disarmament which had formerly been proclaimed. The German Government has no intention of wishing to level a reproach against any State: but today it feels bound to put on record that through the introduction, which has now been decreed, in France of a two-years' period of military service the conceptions which underlay the creation of short-service defensive armies have been abandoned in favour of a long-service organization.

But the short-service system was one of the arguments on which was based the claim that Germany should sacrifice her Reichswehr (Army).

ARMAMENTS FOR DEFENSE

The German Government feels that in these circumstances it is impossible any longer to delay the measures which are necessary for the security of the Reich or indeed to fail to disclose those measures to others.

If therefore the German Government now complies with the wish expressed in the speech of the English Minister Baldwin on 28 November 1934 for information on German intentions it does so

1. In order to give to the German people the conviction and to the other States the knowledge that the safeguarding and security of the German Reich from henceforth will be entrusted to the German nation's own strength. And

2. in order that through fixing the extent of the German

measures it may invalidate all insinuations that the German people is seeking to establish a military hegemony in Europe.

What the German Government, as protector of the honour and interests of the German nation, desires is to secure such a measure of military force as is necessary not merely for maintaining the integrity of the German Reich but also for assuring international respect and esteem for Germany as co-guarantor of general peace.

For at this hour the German Government renews before the

Hitler and Mussolini with German staff officers on August 30,1941

German people and before the entire world the affirmation of its resolve never to go beyond that which the protection of German honour and the freedom of the Reich demand and especially it affirms that it wishes in the national German armament to create no instrument of military aggression, but on the contrary to create exclusively an instrument of defence and therefore an instrument for the maintenance of peace.

The Government of the German Reich further expresses the confident hope that the German people which thus once more finds its way back to its honour may be able in independence and the enjoyment of equal rights to make its contribution to the pacification of the world in free and frank co-operation with the other nations and their Governments.

The League of Nations Is Dead

Benito Mussolini

Between 1934 and 1936, Italy engaged in a series of military operations aimed at conquering and annexing Ethiopia. Italy's actions were in direct violation of Article 10 of the Covenant of the League of Nations, which insured the preservation of the territorial integrity of all member states. A series of sanctions directed toward Italy ultimately proved fruitless. Realizing that the League was not taking any effective action, the government of Italy hastened to ''officially'' annex Ethiopia. On May 9, 1936, the King of Italy decreed that ''the territories and peoples which belonged to the Empire of Ethiopia are placed under the full and entire sovereignty of the Kingdom of Italy. The title of Emperor of Ethiopia is assumed by the King of Italy for himself and his successors.''

In a speech at Milan on November 2, 1936, Benito Mussolini, fascist dictator of Italy, consigned the League to history's graveyard. Emboldened by the conquest of Ethiopia, he implored his fellow *Fascisti* to labor tirelessly for the power and glory of the nation.

Consider the following questions while reading:

1. What examples did Mussolini cite in referring to the illusions of Wilsonian ideology?
2. How did Mussolini suggest that the Italian people ''make a policy of peace''?

Benito Mussolini, **The New York Times**, November 2, 1936. © 1936 by The New York Times Company. Reprinted by permission.

THE ILLUSION OF DISARMAMENT

Blackshirts of Milan: By means of the speech which I am about to make to you and for which I ask, and you will give me, a few dozen minutes of your attention, I intend to to lay down the position of Fascist Italy with regard to its relations with other peoples in this so turgid and disquieting moment.

The high level of your political education allows me to lay before you those problems which elsewhere are debated in so-called Parliaments, even at so-called democratic banquets.

I shall be extremely brief, but I add that every one of my words has been weighed.

THE NOBILITY OF WAR

War alone brings up to its highest tension all human energy, and puts the stamp of nobility upon the peoples who have the courage to meet it. All other trials are substitutes, which never really put men into the position where they have to make the great decision — the alternatives of life or death.

Benito Mussolini, 1935.

If one wishes to clarify the European atmosphere it is first necessary to clear the table of all illusions, of all conventional falsehoods and the lies that still constitute relics of the great shipwreck of Wilsonian ideology.

One of these illusions is already flat, the illusion of disarmament. No one wishes to disarm first, and for all to disarm together is impossible and absurd...

THE ABSURDITY OF THE LEAGUE

For us Fascisti, in the habit of examining with cool eye the reality of life in history, another illusion we reject is that which passed by the name of collective security. Collective security never existed, does not exist, and will never exist. A virile people provides within its borders its collective security and refuses to confide its destiny to uncertain hands of third persons.

Another illusion it is necessary to reject is indivisible peace. Indivisible peace could have only this meaning, indivisible war. Thus, peoples refuse, and justly so, to fight for interests that do not concern them.

The League of Nations is based on the absurdity of the principle of absolute juridical parity among all States; whereas the States are different from one another, at least from the viewpoint of their historic responsibility.

For the League of Nations the dilemma is expressed in very clear terms, either to reform itself or to perish. Since it is extremely difficult for the League to reform itself, as far as we are concerned it can perish in peace.

At any event, we have not forgotten and we will not forget that the League of Nations has organized by methods of diabolical diligence an iniquitous siege against the people of Italy and tried to starve her men, women and children, tried to shatter our military force and the work of civilization being carried on 2,500 to 5,000 miles distant in another land.

It did not succeed, not because it did not want to, but because it found itself faced by the compact unity of the Italian people, capable of all sacrifices and also of fighting the fifty-two coalition States.

THE VALUE OF WAR

The value of war for the political and moral development of mankind has been criticized by large sections of the modern civilized world in a way which threatens to weaken the defensive powers of States by undermining the warlike spirit of the people.

Friedrich A.J. von Bernhardi: **Germany and the Next War**.

Now, in order to make a policy of peace it is not necessary to pass through the corridors of the League of Nations...

THE DUTIES OF FASCISTS

Milan comrades, let us turn to our own affairs: Marching

orders for the fifth year of fascism are the following:

Peace with all, with those near and afar. Armed peace! Therefore, our program of armaments for land, sea and sky will be regularly developed.

Acceleration of all productive energies of the nation, in agricultural and industrial fields. Development of the corporative system to its definite realization.

But here is a duty I confide to you, oh Milanese of this most ardent and most Fascist Milan which has revealed its great soul these days. I confide in you, oh Milanese of this generous working and untiring Milan, this duty:

You must place yourselves, as you will place yourselves, as an advance guard for the development of the empire so as to make it in the shortest possible period an element of well being, of power, of glory for the nation.

Mussolini in his armoured train, 1943

United Press International, Inc.

Identifying Ethnocentrism

Ethnocentrism is the tendency for a group of people to feel that their race or culture is superior to all others and to judge others according to their own frame of reference. A person's **frame of reference** is composed of the standards and values he or she accepts because of his or her life experience and culture. A Marxist in Russia, for example, is likely to view things differently than a Christian in France.

Ethnocentrism has promoted much misunderstanding and conflict throughout the world. It helps emphasize cultural differences and the notion that one nation's institutions are superior to another's. Educators must stress the similarities of the human condition throughout the world and the basic equality and dignity of all people.

In order to avoid war and violence, people must realize how **ethnocentrism** and **frame of reference** limit their abilities to be objective and understanding. Consider each of the following statements carefully. Mark (E) by those statements you think are ethnocentric. Mark (N) by those statements you think are not ethnocentric. Mark (U) if you are undecided.

> E = Ethnocentric
> N = Not Ethnocentric
> U = Undecided

_____ 1. Both the evils and benefits of communism have been exaggerated.

_____ 2. The communists are a menace to our nation and the world.

_____ 3. Some ideals of communism are worth working for.

_____ 4. Communists try to destroy the family and the home.

_____ 5. People should be for their country, right or wrong.

_____ 6. I love to visit foreign countries but I want to live in the United States.

_____ 7. Some people abroad hate the U.S. because they are jealous of our greatness.

_____ 8. The American people are perhaps the finest in the world.

_____ 9. Loyalty to one's country should not take precedence over loyalty to one's moral principles.

_____ 10. The United States comes closer than any nation to being an ideal country.

_____ 11. People should think in terms of being world citizens rather than citizens of a particular country.

_____ 12. The American ideals of bigness, speed, and growth are not suited to the needs of many countries.

_____ 13. The United States is in most ways the greatest nation on earth.

_____ 14. People should not feel any special pride in being identified with Brazil.

_____ 15. There are very few things in the United States that I would want to change.

_____ 16. I feel that the United States is just as selfish as other countries.

_____ 17. Only impractical idealists think that international cooperation can accomplish anything in international relations.

_____ 18. Democratic nations as a rule do not start wars.

_____ 19. We should be willing to fight for the United States whether it is in the right or in the wrong.

Chapter **3**

Internationalism

The United Nations:
Today's Path to Peace?

Viewpoints:
Preamble to The Charter of the United Nations

''And they shall beat their swords into plowshares,
and their spears into pruning hooks;
nation shall not lift up sword against nation,
neither shall they learn war any more.''   Isaiah 2:4 RSV

PREAMBLE TO THE CHARTER OF THE UNITED NATIONS

WE THE PEOPLES OF THE UNITED NATIONS DETERMINED

to save succeeding generations from the scourge of war, which twice in our lifetime has brought untold sorrow to mankind, and

to reaffirm faith in fundamental human rights, in the dignity and worth of the human person, in the equal rights of men and women and of nations large and small, and

to establish conditions under which justice and respect for the obligations arising from treaties and other sources of international law can be maintained, and

to promote social progress and better standards of life in larger freedom,

AND FOR THESE ENDS

to practice tolerance and live together in peace with one another as good neighbors, and

To unite our strength to maintain international peace and security, and

to ensure, by the acceptance of principles and the institution of methods, that armed force shall not be used, save in the common interest, and

to employ international machinery for the promotion of the economic and social advancement of all peoples,

HAVE RESOLVED TO COMBINE OUR EFFORTS TO ACCOMPLISH THESE AIMS.

Accordingly, our respective Governments, through representatives assembled in the city of San Francisco, who have exhibited their full powers found to be in good and due form, have agreed to the present Charter of the United Nations and do hereby establish an international organization to be known as the United Nations.

Viewpoint 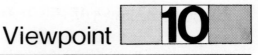 **10**

The United Nations Can Promote Harmony Among Nations

Russell D. Brackett

An educator and author, Russell D. Brackett
has written extensively in the areas of inter-
national affairs and intercultural education.
Brackett is a Minnesota resident who served as
a board member of the Minnesota World Affairs
Center and the Minnesota United Nations
Association. From 1949 to 1956, he headed the
Minneapolis Public School Commission on
International Understanding and World Peace.
He is currently a member of the Advisory
Committee of the United World Federalists.

Consider the following questions while reading:

1. Why does the author claim that the United Nations is "a
   sheer necessity"?
2. How does the author relate American aid to the United
   Nations?

Russell D. Brackett, **Pathways to Peace**, (Minneapolis: T. S. Denison & Company, 1965), pp.
69-72. Reprinted by permission.

A RAPIDLY CHANGING WORLD

The world of the mid-twentieth century bears small resemblance to the same world a hundred or even fifty years earlier. Change, often coming with annoying swiftness, is perhaps the only certainty of this space age. The inevitability of change makes each new decade different from the preceding one.

The fundamental changes that focus the attention of the world's millions on the need for a working instrument of law and order at the international level are several. Among the more obvious changes are the following:

1. The once formidable protection offered a lucky few nations by wide bodies of water and rugged mountain ranges exists no more. Man's ability to make faster than sound flight over celestial thoroughfares has obliterated the former effectiveness of massive physical barriers. No physical environmental mass anywhere today provides man natural protection. An international U.N. police force might be the best substitute.

2. Increasingly the people of the world are realizing the depth and extent of man's interdependence economically, socially and geographically. The availability of mass air communication in the mid-twentieth century accentuates this interdependence. The United Nations is but the political manifestation of this closely knit world.

Just as no man lives alone, so no nation can live unto itself. Albert Einstein said, ''Today no man is an island: Our fate is linked with that of our fellow man throughout the world.''

3. The unbelievably rapid, almost fantastic development of air transportation, stimulated by global wars and man's desire to explore space, has surely knit the world together in one communication fabric as it has never been tied before. A. T. & T.'s Telestar added a new dimension in 1964 to the world of communication.

Alan Shepard in May 1961, climbed into his Mercury capsule atop a fuming Redstone Missile. In his fifteen-minute space ride, Shepard set the tone of travel for the new decade. In years ahead, space will all but surrender to man's ingenuity. The earth, mysterious and unknown to eighteenth century explorers sailing for months to reach an unknown destination, today seems so small. Jules Verne's novel "Around the World in Eighty Days," was long ago old-fashioned and as out of date as Henry Ford's Model T. Time will have new meaning when observing manned satellites circling the world every hour or two becomes a nightly occurrence...

THE U.N. IN TODAY'S WORLD

This ever-changing world demands new kinds of controls. The U.N. must stand by.

4. The age of nuclear weapons with its ugly portent of massive death and destruction on a scale yet undreamed of, focuses man's attention on his need for international agreement, controlling disarmament under a stronger United Nations.

LAST HOPE FOR PEACE

The peoples of the earth turn to the United Nations as the last hope of concord and peace; we presume to present here, with their tribute of honor and of hope, our own tribute also...

The edifice which you have constructed must never fall; it must be perfected and made equal to the needs which world history will permit.

Pope Paul, Address before U.N. General Assembly, October 4, 1965.

In a world of sovereign powers armed with weapons of total destruction, the world's people, in a Churchillian phrase, are "roaming and peering around on the rim of hell."

International organization control of armaments is clearly indicated. Does any international organization exist except the U.N. under whose surveillance this might be accomplished? The United Nations becomes a sheer necessity.

5. Not only is nuclear war unthinkable, but the burden of today's arms cost is intolerably heavy. No sacrifice, for sure, is

too great to protect the national interest under any conditions if there are no alternatives. But dreamy realists in every nation are hoping for the day when but a fraction of the fifty billion currently spent for defense can be diverted preferably through the U.N. to constructive, not destructive, uses. Improving health, raising educational levels, relieving areas of poverty, all problems plaguing over half the world's population, should be the U.N.'s top priority of business, granted the necessary financial resources. These resources might more easily be available were freedom granted from the currently excessive burden of defense spending. An effective limitation and reduction of national armaments would open the door to the solution of these depressing global humanitarian problems. Only the U.N. is available to help open this door...

PEACE FLAG OR BATTLE FLAGS?

Justus in the **Minneapolis Star**. Reprinted by permission.

THE U.N. AND THE COMMON GOOD

6. Wholly on the positive side and for compelling reasons, men of good will everywhere, and they are legion, want to share the good things of life both materially and spiritually. Except through international organization how can the principle of the "common good" be applied to international society?

Former President Eisenhower put it this way: *"Every bomb we can manufacture, every plane, every ship, every gun, in the long run has no purpose other than negative — to give us time to prevent the other fellow from starting a war, since we know we won't. The billions we pour into munitions ought to be supported by a great American effort, a positive constructive effort that leads directly toward what we all want: a true and lasting peace."*

Working through the U.N., American aid hopefully might support an integrated international attack on the world's major ills. What higher motive than peace can be mustered in defense of the U.N.?

POPE JOHN AND THE U.N.

On April 10, 1963, Pope John, speaking to Catholics and non-Catholics alike, indicated he hoped the United Nations eventually might become a strong world authority. The Pope said it was his "earnest wish" that the United Nations be given structure and means to safeguard peace. A supra-national authority must be considered, the Pope added, because national leaders in the modern world are "on a footing of equality" and are "no longer capable of facing the task of finding an adequate solution to the problems."

In Summary:

The United Nations appears to be the best mechanism yet devised for bringing into harmony the conflicting desires of nations in order to maintain peace and security.

The United Nations Promotes Conflict Among Nations

Abraham Yeselson

Chairman of the Department of Political Science at Rutgers University, Abraham Yeselson has researched extensively the role of the United Nations in the maintenance of the international peace and security. He is a specialist in Foreign Relations and has both taught abroad and conducted numerous international seminars. His publications include *A Dangerous Place: United Nations as a Weapon in International Politics.* The following testimony was delivered by Dr. Yeselson at a hearing before the Senate Committee On Foreign Relations on May 8, 1975.

Consider the following questions while reading:

1. What, in the author's opinion, is the correct way to evaluate the United Nations?
2. How does the author suggest that American officials respond to the practices of the United Nations?

From testimony delivered by Dr. Abraham Yeselson before the Senate Committee on Foreign Relations on May 8, 1975.

IS THE U.N. WORKING?

Over a long period of time I began to question the knowledge which had been imparted to me and the theories upon which they were based and I came out in a very funny place in a very uncomfortable place. I came out in a place which says in effect that the proper approach to the United Nations is not from the aspect of the ideals of the Charter or the principles of the organization, but that in order to understand what happens there and how the organization is used, and especially its impact on conflict, it's necessary to approach the organization from the point of view of the motivation of those who use the organization. It took me, perhaps because I am slow, some 15 years to ask a new question. The new question was, ''who brings what issues to the United Nations and why?''

And from that perspective those explanations for what happened at the United Nations acquired a completely different meaning. I understood things better and I believe that I now have the basis for really analyzing how the United Nations contributes to conflict.

From this point of view I answer your fundamental question by saying, yes, the United Nations is working but it is not working for advancing the purposes of the Charter, the principles of the organization, and it is not working in the interests of American foreign policy.

U.N. ONLY A DREAM

Thirty years ago the U.N. began as the result of a dying President's dream to create an organization that would maintain world peace and help to usher in a new era of enlightenment. That the concept could never be more than a dream has, of course, been proven by events.

De Witt S. Copp in **Human Events**, May 29, 1976.

NATIONAL ISSUES DOMINATE THE U.N.

I am not going to be presumptuous and try to advise you on what American foreign policy should be; but if we view the

United Nations, we see clearly that it is now an instrument for the advancement of the foreign policy of those who can dominate it. The targets of attack are apartheid in South Africa, colonialism in Rhodesia and elsewhere such as Puerto Rico, Israel, and it is also used as a weapon for the advancement of particular economic aproaches to the problems of north and south, rich against poor.

These are the issues which dominate the organization. They will continue to do so. Other issues will be added. The Panama Canal issue, the South Korean issue, retention of American troops there.

I think we can predict if relations become worse between the United States and China, and/or between China and the Soviet Union, that new issues involving China will be introduced —

"A HOUSE DIVIDED AGAINST ITSELF..."

Wood, courtesy of **Richmond New Leader**

Chinese attacks on the Soviet Union in respect to border difficulties, on the United States in respect to Taiwan, perhaps the
British in Hong Kong. In every instance, using various strate-
gies which I cannot detail here, states advance national interests, introducing an issue into the United Nations is always
for the achievement of a conflict purpose. The effect is always
to embitter relations among the States and the impact on the
conflict as a result of the introduction of this weapon is to widen
the conflict and make it more difficult to solve peacefully and
less likely that the dispute will be resolved.

MISUSE OF THE U.N. CHARTER

From my peculiar point of view I find, for example, that the
Middle East conflict is in large part a result of the United
Nations' intervention, and that if peace will be achieved there it
will be achieved in spite of the United Nations.

The same is true in respect to the Koreans. After 25 years of
resolutions at the United Nations, essentially in support of
South Korea, if and when any normalization of relations will be
achieved in the Koreas, it will be accomplished in spite of what
has happened at the United Nations and not because of what
has happened...It is nationalism and sovereignty which
prevent the establishment of a community.

You do not create a community by creating an organization and
saying there are community objectives. If the community does
not exist, they will use the organization for selfish purposes in
the name of principles stated in the Charter, and that I think is
precisely what has happened...

WHAT THE UNITED STATES SHOULD DO

Obviously, this government faces hard problems. We romanti-
cized the role of the United Nations and majority rule,
especially when the Organization implemented American
foreign policy. It will be extraordinarily difficult now to ration-
alize continued involvement in an Organization which sponsors
wars, passes one-sided or unenforceable resolutions, provides
forums for international insult instead of diplomacy, and is
guilty of the most outrageous examples of selective justice.
Perhaps it will be impossible for the American people to overcome disillusion and they will demand withdrawal from the

world body. Because such action is inimical to our interests and those of world peace, I urge you, Ambassador Daniel Moynihan, and other responsible officials to publicize honestly and soberly the reasons for our continued participation. By recognizing the United Nations as a dangerous weapon, you will be better able to discount its pernicious effects. You will be less discouraged in your support for quiet diplomacy, mediation, efforts to avert nuclear or environmental catastrophes, and contribute better to social and economic justice for the peoples of the world. Clearer perception of the World Organization will facilitate the search for appropriate means of accomplishing these ends, which reality and good sense demand, and which must be pursued in spite of the uses made of the United Nations.

The World Needs the United Nations

Charles W. Yost

A former lecturer on Foreign Policy at the
Columbia University School of International
Affairs (1971-1973), Charles W. Yost has had a
long association with the United Nations. He is
Honorary Co-Chairman of the United Nations
Association and has served in the organization
in many capacities, including Ambassador and
Permanent Representative of the U.S. to the
U.N. (1969-1971). Yost is the author of *The
Insecurity of Nations* (1968) and *The Conduct
and Misconduct of Foreign Affairs* (1971).

Consider the following questions while reading:

1. On what does the author blame the United Nations' current
   ineffectiveness?
2. What does the author see as ''the great paradox and
   dilemma of present-day international relations''?
3. How does the author suggest the United Nations be
   improved?

Charles W. Yost, ''Who Needs The UN?'' The **Christian Science Monitor**, September 2, 1973.
Syndicated column released on September 18, 1973 © Charles W. Yost 1973. Distributed by the
Frye Syndicate, 2 Tudor City Place, N.Y., N.Y. 10017.

U.S. LEADERSHIP SLACKENS

As the 28th General Assembly gets underway, the UN is encountering once more the annual hand-wringing and pious lamentation about its "ineffectiveness."

There is no doubt that the UN is not as successful in the international security field as it was 20 or even 10 years ago. Rare indeed, however, is the critic who points out why.

The UN, in its present state of evolution, is no more than an association of sovereign states which does or does not do what the most powerful of its members want or do not want it to do.

During the first 20 years of its existence its most powerful member, the U.S., provided sufficient leadership, impetus, and resources so that it was remarkably successful even in the controversial security field.

After 1964, however, piqued by America's defeat on the ill-chosen Article 19 issue, by the antipathy of most UN members to the U.S. Vietnam adventure, and by the "irresponsibility" of third-world members reflecting different interests from America's, U.S. commitment and leadership slackened and the UN ship of state drifted into the present doldrums.

COOPERATION NEEDED

The U.S. Congress has itself twice flagrantly violated the UN Charter, once in refusing to pay America's assessed dues to the International Labor Organization and again in obliging the executive to disregard UN sanctions against Rhodesia, for which the U.S. had itself voted.

Secretary-General Waldheim in the introduction to his current annual report has the following to say: "Of course there is infinite room for improvement in the way the UN is used on immediate issues. It would be a far more effective organization, for example, if member states developed the habit of consistently responding to and respecting the decisions and findings of the main organs.

"It would be a more effective organization if member states

were always prepared to put their influence behind the implementation of the decisions of its organs. It would be a more effective organization if the majority of governments of member states were more interested in pursuing long-term international aims, and in providing leadership in the pursuit of those aims, than in using the UN to achieve narrow goals and to protect short-term national interests.''

BEST HOPE FOR PEACE

Twenty-seven years ago, as Emperor of Ethiopia, I mounted the rostrum in Geneva, Switzerland, to address to the League of Nations an appeal for relief from the destruction which has been unleashed against my defenseless nation. I spoke then both to and for the conscience of the world... Today, I stand before the world organization which has succeeded to the mantle discarded by its discredited predecessor. In this body is enshrined the principle of collective security which I unsuccessfully invoked at Geneva. Here, in this Assembly, reposes the best — perhaps the last — hope for the peaceful survival of mankind.

Address by Haile Selassie, Emperor of Ethiopia, to the U.N. General Assembly on October 4, 1963.

TWO CHARACTERISTICS OF THE U.N.

The great paradox and dilemma of present-day international relations is that the world is becoming more and more closely knit and interdependent economically and culturally, but is still appallingly fragmented nationally, administratively, and psychologically.

Mankind is suffering from a massive and dangerous schizophrenia. It will have to concentrate during the remainder of this century on a crash program to resolve this dilemma, on pain of collapsing into a new dark age of anarchy, famine, and conflict.

We see this endeavor being currently pursued through a wide variety of devices and procedures — a series of bilateral and multilateral summit meetings, a proliferating number of regional organizations and regional conferences, separate conferences among developed and developing countries on both political and economic problems.

Almost all of these serve useful purposes and are necessary steps in the direction of better organizing and structuring interdependence. Most of them, however, lack two important qualities which characterize the UN.

The first of these is universality, which of course enormously complicates the process of agreement but which will nonetheless become more and more necessary as more and more problems become global in their incidence and impact. The

HARASSED NURSEMAID

Justus in the **Minneapolis Star**. Reprinted by permission.

second is the institutional quality of the UN and its family of agencies, as contrasted with the ad hoc ups and downs of bilateral or multilateral negotiations and agreements without any institutional framework.

For example, the prospect of coping successfully with global environmental problems is vastly enhanced by the creation of the UN environmental program, with so far very limited powers but with a firm institutional structure, a concrete mandate and a permanent staff devoting its full energies to identifying, monitoring, and proposing solutions to these problems.

BIG POWER LEADERSHIP NEEDED

Surely mankind, and the nations into which it has artificially divided itself, if they are to survive in the wholly new environment which their own proliferation and their own inventions have created, must move more rapidly toward comprehensive and effective international institutions in the political and security as well as in the economic and technological fields.

As far as the UN is concerned, there is nothing wrong with it which could not be cured by a decade of vigorous, honest, and constructive leadership by the big powers, most of all the U.S. Where that leadership is provided, the UN will prosper and serve peoples and governments effectively. Where it is not provided, the UN will stagnate and decay, at the very time when it is most desperately needed.

Viewpoint

The World Must Replace
the United Nations

Thomas A. Lane

Thomas A. Lane is a graduate of the U.S.
Military Academy at West Point. A career
officer, he served in the Army Corps of
Engineers from 1928 until his retirement as a
Major General in 1962. Since then, he has distinguished himself as a syndicated columnist
and an author. His works include *The War for
the World* (1968) and *America on Trial: The
War for Vietnam* (1971).

Consider the following questions while reading:

1. What examples of the United Nations' lawlessness does the
   author cite?
2. Why does the author suggest the U.S. reconsider its commitment to the U.N.?

Thomas A. Lane, "World Must Replace United Nations," **The Wanderer**, November 1, 1973.
Reprinted with permission from **The Wanderer** and Mrs. Thomas A. Lane.

THE LAWLESSNESS OF THE U.N.

On Oct. 5th, 1973, the United Nations gave another example of the nonsense it is all about. This organization, nominally committed to the furtherance of peace through law, has grown increasingly lawless in recent years.

The expulsion of the Republic of China and the substitution of the People's Democratic Republic of China in the Security Council was accomplished in blatant disregard of the UN Charter. What the delegates could not do legally, they did illegally, under cover of the fiction that the issue was one of valid credentials. The UN pretensions of serving the rule of law are patently fraudulent.

Lawlessness begets lawlessness. On Oct. 5th, 1973, the General Assembly voted to reject the credentials of the delegation from South Africa. When the President of the Assembly ruled that the vote did not impair the right of the South Africans to speak, and the South African Foreign Minister rose to do so, about 100 of the 135 delegates left the chamber. This was lawlessness crowned with boorishness. The General Assembly is obviously incapable of maintaining a civilized standard of diplomacy.

A MORE PEACEFUL WORLD

It is time to reconsider the U.S. commitment to the United Nations. The organization was founded on the false premise that the victors of World War II would remain united in their commitment to peace. The Soviet commitment to conquest made a mockery of that hope. In consequence, the United Nations has become not an influence for peace but a cockpit of

GET US OUT!

An all-powerful United Nations would mean sacrificing every principle Americans revere. This is another compelling reason why we are petitioning Congress to Get Us Out! of the U.N. — and why we urge you to support this campaign.

A pamphlet by the John Birch Society.

conflict. It is used by blocs hostile to the United States to further their self-interest. It is a sign of our decrepit foreign policy that we pay what we do to sustain this instrument of our embarrassment.

The world would be a more peaceful place if the United Nations were disbanded. Nations would then be put at some disadvantage to concert their disruptive plans; and their efforts to do so would not be obscured by the screen of a ''peaceful'' assembly.

The rule of law requires a fresh start. It is futile to try to devise a rule acceptable to both Communist and free states. To attempt it is to subvert the principles of freedom with the demands of tyranny. We have seen in twenty-five years of the

THE LADY AND THE TIGER

Justus in the **Minneapolis Star**. Reprinted by permission.

UN organization a steady erosion of the principles of freedom and the substitution of naked power politics on the Communist model. Advantage, not law, governs the conduct of the United Nations.

ABOLISH THE U.N.

A rule of international law can be furthered only by nations philosophically committed to its development. We need a new concert of nations, to include only those committed to standards of law in freedom, on which a new structure of international accord can be based. Membership should be open only to those powers which in their internal structure and international policy give bona fides of their commitment to peace through law. Such a concert of nations might indeed set a new standard of cooperation in the common good. It could do much to sustain and strengthen the rule of law — and by its success, it would become a magnet for other nations of the world.

But, some will ask, why not reform the United Nations? The United Nations cannot be reformed. It has basic and irreformable defects of concept and structure. We must start all over again with a new organization.

Exercise 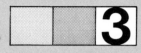 **3**

Determining Priorities

Pretend that you are the Secretary of the Treasury and the President has asked you for a recommendation as to how much money should be spent in the coming fiscal year on the following national problems. Assuming you have a National Budget of 350 billion dollars to work with, how much money would you advise the President to spend on each of the following domestic and foreign items?

$ _____ Foreign Military Aid

$ _____ Energy Research for Solar, Wind, and Geothermal Power

$ _____ Health, Education, and Welfare

$ _____ Foreign Economic Aid

$ _____ Nuclear Energy Research

$ _____ World Economic Cooperation

$ _____ Domestic and Foreign Environmental Concerns

$ _____ World Disarmament

$ _____ Human Rights

$ _____ A World Government with police powers to prevent wars

$ _____ National Defense

Chapter 4

Internationalism

Interdependence:
Tomorrow's Path to Peace?

Viewpoint ▉ **14**

A Declaration of Interdependence

Henry Steele Commager

Henry Steele Commager is one of this century's leading scholars of U.S. history. He received his PhD from the University of Chicago in 1928 and has taught at New York University, Columbia University and Amherst College. Editor of *The Rise of the American Nation*, a projected fifty volume series, his other works include *The Heritage of America; Freedom, Loyalty and Dissent*, and *The American Mind*. The following text (appearing in its entirety) was composed by Commager for the World Affairs Council of Philadelphia and published on United Nations Day, October 24, 1975.

Consider the following questions while reading:

1. What does the author cite as self-evident truths?
2. What challenge does the author extend to the American people?

Henry Steele Commager, ''Declaration of Interdependence,'' **Today's Education**, March 1976, pp. 86-87. Reprinted with permission from **Today's Education** and Henry Steele Commager.

ESTABLISH A NEW WORLD ORDER

When in the course of history the threat of extinction confronts mankind, it is necessary for the people of the United States to declare their interdependence with the people of all nations and to embrace those principles and build those institutions which will enable mankind to survive and civilization to flourish.

Two centuries ago our forefathers brought forth a new nation; now we must join with others to bring forth a new world order. On this historic occasion, it is proper that the American people should reaffirm those principles on which the United States of America was founded, acknowledge the new crises which confront them, accept the new obligations which history imposes upon them, and set forth the causes which impel them to affirm before all peoples their commitment to a Declaration of Interdependence.

HUMANITY IS ONE

We hold these truths to be self-evident: That all men are created equal; that the inequalities and injustices which afflict so much of the human race are the product of history and society, not of God or nature; that people everywhere are entitled to the blessings of life and liberty, peace and security, and the realization of their full potential; that they have an inescapable moral obligation to preserve those rights for posterity; and that to achieve these ends, all the peoples and nations of the globe should acknowledge their interdependence and join together to dedicate their minds and their hearts to the solution of those problems which threaten their survival.

To establish a new world order of compassion, peace, justice, and security, it is essential that mankind free itself from the limitations of national prejudice and acknowledge that the forces that unite it are incomparably deeper than those that divide it — that all people are part of one global community, dependent on one body of resources, bound together by the ties of a common humanity, and associated in a common adventure on the planet Earth.

Let us then join together to vindicate and realize this great truth that mankind is one and, as one, will nobly save or irreparably lose the heritage of thousands of years of civilization.

And let us set forth the principles which should animate and inspire us if our civilization is to survive.

GLOBAL RESOURCES BELONG TO ALL

We affirm that the resources of the globe are finite, not infinite; that they are the heritage of no one nation or generation, but of all peoples and nations and of posterity; and that our deepest obligation is to transmit to that posterity a planet richer in material bounty, in beauty, and in delight that we found it. Narrow notions of national sovereignty must not be permitted to curtail that obligation.

NO MAN IS AN ISLAND

No man is an island, entire of itself; every man is a piece of the continent, a part of the main. If a clod be washed away by the sea, Europe is the less, as well as if a promontory were, as well as if a manor of thy friends or of thine own were. Any man's death diminishes me because I am involved in mankind, and therefore never send to know for whom the bell tolls; it tolls for thee.

John Donne (1572-1631) in Meditation 17.

We affirm that the exploitation of the poor by the rich and of the weak by the strong violates our common humanity and denies to large segments of society the blessings of life, liberty, and happiness. We recognize a moral obligation to strive for a more prudent and more equitable sharing of the resources of the earth in order to ameliorate poverty, hunger, and disease.

We affirm that the resources of nature are sufficient to nourish and sustain all the present inhabitants of the globe and that there is an obligation on every society to distribute those resources equitably, along with a corollary obligation on every society to assure that its population does not place upon nature a burden heavier than it can bear.

COOPERATION IS NECESSARY

We affirm our responsibility to help create conditions which will make for peace and security and to build more effective machinery for keeping peace among the nations. Because the insensate accumulation of nuclear, chemical, and biological weapons threatens the survival of mankind, we call for the immediate reduction and eventual elimination of these weapons under international supervision. We deplore the reliance on force to settle disputes between nation states and between rival groups within such states.

We affirm that the oceans are the common property of mankind, whose dependence on their incomparable resources of nourishment and strength will, in the next century, become crucial for human survival, and that their exploitation should be so regulated as to serve the interests of the entire globe and of future generations.

ATOMIC CLOUD

Justus in the **Minneapolis Star**. Reprinted by permission.

We affirm that pollution flows with the waters and flies with the winds; that it recognizes no boundary lines and penetrates all defenses; that it works irreparable damage alike to nature and to mankind — threatening with extinction the life of the seas, the flora and fauna of the earth, and the health of the people in cities and the countryside alike — and that it can be adequately controlled only through international cooperation.

We affirm that the exploration and utilization of outer space is a matter equally important to all the nations of the globe and that no nation can be permitted to exploit or develop the potentialities of the planetary system exclusively for its own benefit.

We affirm that the economy of all nations is a seamless web and that no one nation can any longer effectively maintain its processes of production and monetary system without recognizing the necessity for collaborative regulation by international authorities.

We affirm that, in a civilized society, the institutions of science and the arts are never at war, and we call upon all nations to exempt these institutions from the claims of chauvinistic nationalism and to foster that great community of learning and creativity whose benign function it is to advance civilization and to further the health and happiness of mankind.

UNITE FOR THE CHALLENGE

We affirm that a world without law is a world without order, and we call upon all nations to strengthen and sustain the United Nations and its specialized agencies and other institutions of world order and to broaden the jurisdiction of the World Court in order that these may preside over a reign of law which will not only end wars but will end as well as the mindless violence that terrorizes our society even in times of peace.

We can no longer afford to make little plans, allow ourselves to be the captives of events and forces over which we have no control, or consult our fears rather than our hopes. We call upon the American people, on the threshold of the third century of our national existence, to display once again that boldness, enterprise, magnanimity, and vision which enabled the founders of our Republic to bring forth a new nation and inaugurate a new era in human history. The fate of humanity hangs in the balance. Throughout the globe, hearts and hopes wait upon us. We summon all mankind to unite to meet the great challenge.

The United States Must Reject Interdependence

Marjorie S. Holt

A 1949 graduate of the University of Florida
School of Law, Marjorie S. Holt practiced law in
Annapolis, Maryland until 1966 when she was
elected to the U.S. House of Representatives.
She has remained active in Maryland politics
both as a member of the League of Women
Voters and as Counsel for the Maryland Federa-
tion of Republican Women.

Consider the following questions while reading:

1. Why does Congresswoman Holt suggest that the American
   people reject the Declaration of Interdependence?
2. Why does Congresswoman Holt feel that the Declaration of
   Interdependence is contrary to American ideals and would
   not aid world peace?

Marjorie S. Holt in a speech delivered in the U.S. House of Representatives on January 19, 1976.

INTERDEPENDENCE MEANS SURRENDER

Many of us recently received a letter from the World Affairs Council of Philadelphia, inviting Members of Congress to participate in a ceremonial signing of ''A Declaration of Interdependence'' on January 30 in Congress Hall, adjacent to Independence Hall in Philadelphia.

A number of Members of Congress have been invited to sign this document, lending their prestige to its theme, but I want the record to show my strong opposition to this declaration.

It calls for surrender of our national sovereignty to international organization. It declares that our economy should be regulated by international authorities. It proposes that we enter a ''new world order'' that would redistribute the wealth created by the American people.

This is an obscenity that defiles our Declaration of Independence, signed 200 years ago in Philadelphia. We fought a great Revolution for independence and individual liberty, but now it is proposed that we participate in a world socialist order.

Are we a proud and free people, or are we a carcass to be picked by the jackals of the world, who want to destroy us?

When one cuts through the highflown rhetoric of this ''Declaration of Interdependence,'' one finds key phrases that tell the story.

For example, it states that: ''The economy of all nations is a seamless web, and that no one action can any longer effectively maintain its processes of production and monetary systems without recognizing the necessity for collaborative regulation by international authorities.''

How do you like the idea of ''international authorities'' controlling our production and our monetary system? How could any American dedicated to our national independence and freedom tolerate such an idea?

INDEPENDENCE AND FREEDOM FOR AMERICA

The declaration goes on to urge a strengthening of the United Nations and a broadening of the jurisdiction of the World

Court, "that these may preside over a reign of law that will not only end wars but end as well the mindless violence which terrorizes our society even in times of peace."

Examine this closely. It suggests that world government will somehow cure the problems of crime and terrorism, not just the problem of war. Quite obviously, the sponsors of this declaration have lost all contact with reality.

We have lately witnessed the United Nations organization in full cry against America and her allies of the Free World. We have watched the U.N. become an instrument of the Soviet Union and its shabby following of despots large and small.

America should never subject her fate to decisions by such an assembly, unless we long for national suicide. Instead, let us have independence and freedom.

A BETRAYAL OF IDEALS

If we surrender our independence to a "new world order" dominated by the Soviet Union and its clients, we will be betraying our historic ideals of freedom and self-government.

Dwight D. Eisenhower, in a speech to the General Assembly of the U.N., September 22, 1960.

A major threat to world peace is the Soviet Union, which imposes slavery on its people and devotes its economy to the single task of building a war machine to extend that slavery throughout the world.

It subverts governments of independent nations; it arms and impels its subservient client states to wage wars of conquest against their neighbors.

AMERICA MUST REMAIN POWERFUL

There is one force that preserves freedom where it still survives in this world, and that is the strength of the United States. To the extent that we maintain a powerful, credible economic and military deterrent, we shall also have peace.

The Soviet Union seeks world empire. America asks only that

free peoples remain unmolested by the slavemasters of the Kremlin.

If we resist the expansion of the empire that threatens to dominate the world and destroy the independence of every nation, we shall be fulfilling the ideas of our Declaration of Independence.

If we surrender our independence to a "new world order" dominated by the Soviet Union and its clients, we will be betraying our historic ideals of freedom and self-government.

Freedom and self-government are not outdated. The fathers of our Republic fought a revolution for those ideals, which are as valid today as they ever were.

Let us not betray freedom by embracing slavemasters; let us not betray self-government with world government; let us celebrate Jefferson and Madison, not Marx and Lenin.

World Federalism
Is Possible

Norman Cousins

Editor of the *Saturday Review* since 1942,
Norman Cousins is a world recognized spokes-
person for Internationalism. He was a member
of the Commission to Study Organized Peace,
founder and president of the United World
Federalists and co-chairman of the National
Committee for a Sane Nuclear Policy. Cousins
has labored tirelessly for the cause of world
peace through world government and has
authored numerous books on the subject
including *Modern Man is Obsolete* and *In Place
of Folly*.

Consider the following questions while reading:

1. What does the author claim was the American Founding
   Fathers' main contribution to history?
2. How does the author compare the American situation
   between 1783 and 1789 to the current world situation?

Norman Cousins, ''Reflections on a Birthday,'' **Saturday Review**. Reprinted with permission
from **Saturday Review** and Norman Cousins.

THE U.S. CONSTITUTION

The range of America's contribution to history...runs broad
and deep, but the idea that ultimately may have the single
greatest impact on the world is that human beings are capable
of designing a rational future. The specific expression of that
capability in this nation was the United States Constitution.
This country was not the first in history to devise a representative government, but no other society was more carefully
constructed for the express purpose of making representative
government work.

The fact that the United States has lived longer under a single
continuous form of government than has any other major
nation is a tribute to that design. The U.S. Constitution was a
piece of political architecture specifically intended to with-
stand the stresses and flaws that throughout history had
caused other governments to become erratic or irresponsible or
to turn against their own people. The American idea that
government could be constructed as an act of intelligence and
free will has inspired countless peoples and has produced more
change in the world than any other political or even ideological
concept, not excluding Marxism.

DIFFICULTIES IN EARLY AMERICA

The design of the young American Founding Fathers was not
struck off overnight. It took two years to hammer out that
design and to put it into effect. Each problem and challenge
had to be examined in the light of historical experience and
common sense. Failures of previous governments became the
raw materials for constructing a durable new model. Of all
these failures, none was more dramatic, significant, or in-
sistent than the collapse of the American states themselves in
their ill-fated experience before federation.

This failure, indeed, was to serve as the impetus for the
enduring structure that became the United States; but the fact
and implications of that failure are not generally understood
today by Americans themselves.

The popular notion about the origin of the United States
government is that the Declaration of Independence and the
United States Constitution were part of a single historical

process. This misconception is reflected in the Bicentennial celebration itself. The United States will not be 200 years old in 1976. The United States was not born until 1789. The nation will not have its Bicentennial until 1989. This is not a historical quibble. There were years of deterioration and disintegration after the end of the Revolution before the U.S. Constitution came into being.

Before the United States could be born, the 13 sovereign American governments had to undergo a collapse of mammoth proportions. John Fiske, in *The Critical Period of American History, 1783-1789*, has written a sobering account of this collapse. The 13 states thought they could retain predominant sovereignty and still be at peace with one another. After 1783, when the treaty was signed with England, the American states slid into a period of disruption bordering on anarchy. New York and New Jersey shot it out in the harbor over the right to tax incoming ships. Pennsylvania and New Jersey never could agree on a mutually satisfactory border. Connecticut and Massachusetts were at odds over the acquisition of western territories. The value of a citizen's currency would shrink 10 percent when he or she crossed a state line. Thus a citizen who started out from New Hampshire with $100 in his pocket would have $20.24 left by the time he arrived in Georgia — without having spent a cent.

A FEDERAL SYSTEM OF GOVERNMENT

Men of reason were convinced that it was a fallacy to suppose that 13 separate sovereign states could exist within a compressed geographic unit. They came together at Philadelphia in 1787 because the situation confronting the states was intolerable. They had no way of knowing whether they could create a new design acceptable to each of the separate states. But they hoped that the results of their efforts might produce a groundswell of popular support that would create an imperative for ratification by the individual legislatures.

The most distinctive feature of the document created at Philadelphia was its federalist principles. The individual states retained jurisdiction over their own territories while yielding authority on all matters concerned with common dangers and common needs. This meant that a central authority spoke and acted for all the states in their collective relationship to the rest of the world.

The main contribution to history of the American Founding Fathers, therefore, was their delineation of the principles by which peace among sovereign units could be created and maintained. They had studied the basic causes of war all the way back to the conflict between Athens and Sparta. They understood the imperatives of geography. They knew that the freedoms of the individual would erode without a structured framework of order for society itself.

UNITY IN FREEDOM

In urging progress toward a world community, I cite the American concept of the destiny of a progressive society. Here in this land, in what was once a wilderness, we have generated a society and a civilization drawn from many sources. Yet out of the mixture of many peoples and faiths we have developed unity in freedom — a unity designed to protect the rights of each individual while enhancing the freedom and well-being of all.

This concept of unity in freedom, drawn from the diversity of many racial strains and cultures, we would like to see made a reality for all mankind...

Thus we see as our goal, not a superstate above nations but a world community embracing them all, rooted in law and justice and enhancing the potentialities and common purposes of all peoples.

Dwight D. Eisenhower, in a speech to the General Assembly of the U.N., September 22, 1960.

WORLD-WIDE FEDERALISM

The fact that our national Bicentennial birthday is not in 1976 but in 1989 is not so important as our ability to understand the principles that went into the making of this nation. Those principles are no less valid now than they were 200 years ago. The peace of the world today is precarious because many of the sovereign units, especially the major ones, are unwilling to accept, or even to consider, the principles that alone can establish workable world order and thus guarantee their peace and independence. The United States, against the background of its history and traditions, has a natural reason to proclaim these principles. We can perform a great service to ourselves and to the cause of world peace by refuting the notion that the highest value is absolute national sovereignty. We can carry the banner for the idea that world peace cannot be achieved, nor the natural rights of human beings protected and enlarged, without a genuine world order.

It will be said that to draw a parallel between the failures of the American states from 1783 to 1787 and the United Nations' situation today is to overstretch historical analogy. It will be claimed that the hundreds or so sovereignties in the present world are too diffuse, too farflung, too complex, to be compared with the 13 states. But one can almost hear James Madison or Alexander Hamilton saying, as they did in *The Federalist Papers*, that historical principles transcend the size and complexity of the case at hand. The larger the problem, they said, the more pertinent the principle. And the principle that informed their efforts at Philadelphia, and that has meaning for us today, is that the only way to eliminate anarchy is by establishing law. They would say that the only security for Americans today, or for any people, is in the creation of a system of world order that enables nations to retain sovereignty over their cultures and institutions but that creates a workable authority for regulating the behavior of the nations in their relationships with one another. They would recognize the mountainous complexities to be surmounted, but they would also believe that there are nuclear imperatives which dictate the need for world law.

World federalism may seem too remote a goal to serve as the basis for immediate efforts. But a world that is ingenious enough to create the means of nuclear incineration ought to be resourceful enough to devise a way out with a time schedule to match.

World Federalism
Will Not Work

G. Edward Griffin

A conservative writer and graduate of the
University of Michigan, G. Edward Griffin has
lectured throughout the U.S. in opposition to
the United Nations and America's membership
in the world body. He has worked in television,
film production, and public relations, and has
authored *The Life and Words of Robert Welch,
Founder of the John Birch Society* and *The
Fearful Master*.

Consider the following questions while reading:

1. Why does the author claim that America's success with
   federalism does not guarantee the success of world
   federalism?
2. How does the author think world peace can be best realized?

G. Edward Griffin, **The Fearful Master: A Second Look at the United Nations**, (Belmont:
Western Islands Publishing Co., 1964), pp. 225-27. Reprinted by permission of the publisher,
Western Islands, Belmont, Massachusetts 02178.

THE U.N. AND THE THIRTEEN COLONIES

The UN is merely doing between nations what we did so successfully with our thirteen colonies. This, in essence, is the plea for federalism, and is based on the idea that the mere act of joining separate political units together into a larger federal entity will somehow prevent those units from waging war with each other. The success of our own federal system is most often cited as proof that this theory is valid. But such an evaluation is a shallow one. First of all, the American Civil War, one of the most bloody in all history, illustrates conclusively that the mere federation of governments, even those culturally similar, as in America, does not automatically prevent war between them. Secondly, we find that true peace quite easily exists between nations which are *not* federated. As a matter of fact, members of the British Commonwealth of Nations seemed to get along far more peacefully after the political bonds between them had been relaxed. In other words, true peace has absolutely nothing to do with whether separate political units are joined together — except, perhaps, that such a union may create a common military defense sufficiently impressive to deter an aggressive attack. But that is peace between the union and outside powers; it has little effect on peace between the units, themselves, which is the substance of the UN argument.

INCREASING THE DANGER OF WAR

In the United Nations, there are precious few common bonds that could help overcome the clash of cross-purposes that inevitably must arise between groups with such divergent ethnic, linguistic, legal, religious, cultural and political environments. To add fuel to the fire, the UN concept is one of unlimited governmental power to impose by force a monolithic set of values and conduct on all groups and individuals whether they like it or not. Far from insuring peace, such conditions can only enhance the chances of war.

FEDERALISM: TYRANNY OF THE MAJORITY

Peace is the natural result of relationships between groups and cultures which are mutually satisfactory to both sides. These relationships are found with equal ease within or across federal lines. As a matter of fact, they are the same relationships that promote peaceful conditions within the community, the neighborhood, the family itself. What are they? Just stop and think for a moment; if you were marooned on an island with two other people, what relationships between you would be mutually satisfactory enough to prevent you from resorting to violence in your relationships? Or, to put it the other way around, what would cause you to break the peace and raise your hand against your partners?

Obviously, if one or both of the others attempted to seize your food and shelter, you would fight. Their reaction to similar efforts on your part would be the same. If they attempted to take away your freedom, to dictate how you should conduct your affairs, or tell you what moral and ethical standards you must follow, likewise, you would fight. And if they constantly ridiculed your attire, your manners and your speech, in time you might be sparked into a brawl. The best way to keep the peace on that island is for each one to mind his own business, to respect each other's right to his own property, to respect the other fellow's right to be different (even to act in a way that seems foolish or improper, if he wishes), to have compassion for each other's troubles and hardships — but to *force* each other to do nothing! And, to make sure that the others hold to their end of the bargain, each should keep physically strong enough to make any violation of this code unprofitable.

Now, suppose these three got together and decided to form a political union, to "federate," as it were. Would this really change anything? Suppose they declared themselves to be the United Persons, and wrote a charter, and held daily meetings, and passed resolutions. What then? These superficial ceremonies might be fun for a while, but the minute two of them out-voted the other, and started "legally" to take his food and shelter, limit his freedom, or force him to accept an unwanted standard of moral conduct, they would be right back where they all began. Charter or no charter they would fight.

Is it really different between nations? Not at all. The same simple code of conduct applies in all human relationships, large or small. Regardless of the size, be it international or three men on an island, the basic unit is still the human personality.

Ignore this fact, and any plan is doomed to failure.

COLONIAL AMERICA AND THE U.N.

When the thirteen colonies formed our Federal Union, they had two very important factors in their favor, neither of which are present in the United Nations. First, the colonies themselves were all of a similar cultural background. They enjoyed similar legal systems, they spoke the same language, and they shared similar religous beliefs. They had much in common. The second advantage, and the most important of the two, was that they formed their union under a constitution which was designed to prevent any of them, *or a majority of them*, from forcefully intervening in the affairs of the others. The original federal government was authorized to provide mutual defense, run a post office, and that was about all. As previously mentioned, however, even though we had these powerful forces working in our favor, full scale war did break out at one tragic point in our history.

The peace that followed, of course, was no peace at all, but was only the smoldering resentment and hatred that falls in the wake of any armed conflict. Fortunately, the common ties between North and South, the cultural similarities and the common heritage, have proved through the intervening years to overbalance the differences. And with the gradual passing away of the generation that carried the battle scars, the Union has healed.

In the United Nations, there are precious few common bonds that could help overcome the clash of cross-purposes that inevitably must arise between groups with such divergent ethnic, linguistic, legal, religious, cultural and political environments. To add fuel to the fire, the UN concept is one of unlimited governmental power to impose by force a monolithic set of values and conduct on all groups and individuals whether they like it or not. Far from insuring peace, such conditions can only enhance the chances of war.

Distinguishing Between Statements That Are Provable and Those That Are Not

From various sources of information, we are constantly confronted with statements and generalizations about social and moral problems. In order to think clearly about these problems, it is useful if one can distinguish between statements which can be verified and those which cannot because evidence is not available, or because the issue is so controversial that it cannot be definitely proved. Students should constantly be aware that social studies texts and other sources often contain statements of a controversial nature. The following exercise is designed to allow you to experiment with statements that are provable and those that are not.

For each of the following statements, indicate whether you believe it is provable (P), too controversial to be proved to everyone's satisfaction (C), or unprovable because of the lack of evidence (U). Compare and discuss your results with your classmates.

P = Provable
C = Too Controversial
U = Unprovable

___ 1. Any person who loves people should refuse to engage in any war.

___ 2. Democratic countries have at times been imperialistic and aggressive in their behavior toward other nations.

___ 3. Patriotism is the most important characteristic of good citizenship.

___ 4. People should regard themselves more as citizens of the world than as citizens of a single country.

___ 5. The United Nations Charter says that all U.N. member nations can also be members of the U.N. Security Council.

___ 6. People are happier in democratic societies.

___ 7. The American military budget should be cut by at least twenty per cent.

___ 8. Americans are a mixture of all nationalities.

___ 9. The United States should not try to be friendly toward communist countries.

___ 10. We must make an effort to be friendly toward all nations.

___ 11. The communist nations are the only major obstacle to world peace.

___ 12. American foreign policy places too much emphasis on military force and not enough on political negotiations and economic aid.

___ 13. The United States must always be the most powerful nation on earth.

___ 14. The United States is stronger militarily than the Soviet Union.

___ 15. The United States and the Soviet Union must both accept military parity with each other if meaningful negotiations to reduce nuclear and conventional arms are to eventually succeed.

Selected Bibliography

WORLD GOVERNMENT

Norman Cousins   Thought for the New Year; Proposal for World Federalism. *Saturday Review*, December 24, 1966, p. 28.

Gerald R. Ford   International Partnership to Improve Tomorrow's World. *Department of State Bulletin*, April 7, 1975, pp. 429-434.

H. K. Jacobson   Structuring the Global System: American Contributions to International Organization. *Annals of the American Academy of Political and Social Science*, 428, (November 1976): 77-90.

D. P. Moynihan   Party and International Politics. *Commentary*, 63, (February 1977): 56-59.

M. Viorst   Promoting the Dream; World Peace Through Law. *Saturday Review World*, November 6, 1973, pp. 10-11.

Christian Century   Wane and Wax of Isolationism. November 10, 1971, pp. 13-15.

Percy E. Corbett   *The Growth of World Law*. Princeton, New Jersey: Princeton University Press, 1971.

Norman Cousins   *Modern Man Is Obsolete*. New York: The Viking Press, 1945.

William O. Douglas   *Towards a Global Federalism*. New York: New York University Press, 1968.

Ernst B. Haas   *Beyond the Nation-State*. Stanford, California: Stanford University Press, 1964.

LEAGUE OF NATIONS

B. D. Allinson   Life or Death for the League. *Nation*, November 4, 1925, p. 511.

D. Borden-Turner	League of Nations and the International Movement. *Contemporary Review*, 124, (September 1923): 350-354.
H. N. Braelsford	League of Nations: A Misprint in History. *Nation*, February 2, 1927, pp. 111-113.
R. Cecil	Case for the League. *Living Age*, December 15, 1923, pp. 491-496.
H. Feis	Successful League of Nations: The Basis of European Security. *Annals of the American Academy of Political and Social Science*, 126, (July 1926): 65-67.
W. Irwin	Did the League of Nations Fail? *Collier's*, November 3, 1923, p. 13.
L. P. Jacks	League of Nations Or a League of Governments? *Atlantic Monthly*, 131, (February 1923): 161-171.
S. Lauzanne	League of Nations: A World Court or World Club? *Living Age*, December 8, 1923, pp. 443-447.
Literary Digest	Living Argument for the League. April 14, 1923, pp. 12-13.
T. Marburg	International Decency. *Forum*, 68, (July 1922): 613-623.
W. Martin	Has the League Done Its Duty? *Living Age*, July 15, 1927, pp. 1053-1056.
S. Rice	Problems of the League. *Fortune*, 121, (May 1924): 647-660.

Sherrill E. Aberg	*Wilson and the League: Why was a Just Cause Defeated?* New York: Scholastic Book Services, 1966.
Philip J. Baker	*League of Nations: Protocol for the Pacific Settlement of International Disputes*. London: P.S. King and Son, 1925.
Samuel Colcord	*Great Deception*. New York: Boni and Lineright, 1921.

THE UNITED NATIONS

D. Abshire

Is the U.N. Committing Suicide? *Readers Digest*, 108, (March 1976): 173-174 + .

Christian Century

U.N.'s Disastrous Situation. November 24, 1971, p. 1373.

G. J. Heeht

United Nations: Looking Forward with Hope. *Parents Magazine*, 45, (October 1970): 27.

H. A. Jack

Terrorism: Another U.N. Failure. *America*, October 20, 1973, pp. 282-285.

D. Lawrence

Making the U.N. Effective. *U.S. News and World Report*, September 28, 1970, p. 92.

Life

How Relevant is the U.N.? May 8, 1970, p. 48.

J. Scali

United Nations: Instrument for International Cooperation. *Department of State Bulletin*, December 3, 1973, pp. 682-687.

J. J. Sisco

Hard Work Ahead for the United Nations. *Department of State Bulletin*, April 11, 1966, pp. 571-576.

K. W. Thompson

United Nations on a Divided Planet. *Saturday Review*, March 19, 1966, pp. 41-42.

A. Tuckerman

U.N. at Thirty: More than an Echo Chamber. *Nation*, November 2, 1974, pp. 425-428.

U.S. News & World Report

Does the United Nations Have a Future? February 28, 1966, pp. 72-74.

U.S. News & World Report

U.N.: A Quarter Century of What? July 8, 1970, p. 40.

Otto von Habsburg

Let's Change Our Tactics in the U.N. *Saturday Evening Post*, 247, (September 1975): 18 + .

C. W. Yost

Whose United Nations? *New Republic*, February 1, 1975, p. 33.

INTERDEPENDENCE

A. N. Gilbert   International Relations and the Spirit of Tragedy.
                     Yale Review, 60, (October 1970): 45-52.

D. Lawrence   Missing Brotherhood. *U.S. News and World Report*,
                     March 14, 1966, p. 120.

D. Mattern   World in Re-Birth? *Catholic World*, 213, (July 1971):
                     139-143.

New Yorker   Interdependence. July 28, 1975, p. 17.

New Yorker   Notes and Comment; Interdependence of Countries.
                     January 7, 1974, pp. 21.

J. J. Sisco   Rising Hopes for International Cooperation.
                     Department of State Bulletin, September 26, 1966,
                     pp. 458-463.

K. Waldheim   Toward Global Interdependence. *Saturday Review
                     World*, August 24, 1974, pp. 63-64.

C. Yost   Letter to a Soviet Friend. *Life*, September 24, 1971,
                     p. 4.

J.E.S. Fawcett   *The Law of Nations*. New York: Basic Books Inc.,
                     1968.

F. H. Hinsley   *Power and the Pursuit of Peace*. Cambridge:
                     University Press, 1963.

Lester Pearson   *Peace in the Family of Man*. Toronto: Oxford
                     University Press, 1969.

John H. Randall   *World Community; the Supreme Task of the
                     Twentieth Century*. New York: Stokes, 1930.

The Editor

BRUNO LEONE received his B.A. (Phi Kappa Phi) from Arizona State University and his M.A. in history from the University of Minnesota. A Woodrow Wilson Fellow (1967), he is currently an instructor at Metropolitan Community College, Minneapolis, where he has taught history, anthropology, and political science. In 1974-75, he was awarded a Fellowship by the National Endowment for the Humanities to research the intellectual origins of American Democracy.

SERIES EDITORS

GARY E. McCUEN received his A.B. degree in history from Ripon College. He also has an M.S.T. degree in history from Wisconsin State University in Eau Claire, Wisconsin. He has taught social studies at the high school level and is co-originator of the *Opposing Viewpoints Series*, *Future Planning Game Series*, *Photo Study Cards* and *Opposing Viewpoints Cassettes*. He is currently working on new materials to be published by Greenhaven Press.

DAVID L. BENDER is a history graduate from the University of Minnesota. He also has an M.A. in government from St. Mary's University in San Antonio, Texas. He has taught social problems at the high school level and is a co-originator of the *Opposing Viewpoints Series*, *Future Planning Game Series*, *Photo Study Cards* and *Opposing Viewpoints Cassettes*. He is currently working on new materials that will be published by Greenhaven Press.